Praise for BACKWARDS

"*Backwards Off the Curb* poetic images resonate to the core. Chris McMillan takes us on a woman's journey through challenging territories of diverse emotional terrain. She pioneers a vision that is as extraordinary as it is practical. Her girlhood imagination, fertilized in the rural south, offers readers rich soil to locate and grow their own dreams. McMillan's authentic style grounds her readers and invites us to travel with her to learn what it means to leave home and return again, this time with a bigger heart and fresh eyes."
~ Jennifer Manlowe,
author of *Writing From Life, Loving Life As It Is*
and *Cracking Up: How Good Girrrls Go Bad*

"Chris McMillan is a wonderful storyteller! Her candor and the clarity of her writing are deeply engaging: her readers join her as she tries to unravel the knots and re-weave the fabric of her life. Hers is a classic but very particular woman's journey of truth-seeking—difficult, stubborn, mysterious and relentless. Readers will be fascinated, encouraged, blessed."
~ Elaine Prevallet SL,
author of *Toward a Global Spirituality, Interconnections, Reflections on Simplicity*, and contributor to *Weavings*

"Chris McMillan is a fine story teller with a well honed sense for weaving remembrance and self-reflection. I have smiled often and winced equally at her capacity to name the unspoken truths that inhabit both the family story and the personal psyche. This is not a story for those who wish to be entertained in order to avoid the realities of the human condition. This is a story that stirs one into asking those forbidden questions of oneself that lead to a deeper appreciation for the history that leads us into a sense of celebration for our "one and precious life.""
~ Paula M. Reeves,
author of *Women's Intuition: Unlocking the Wisdom of the Body*
and *Heart Sense: Unlocking Your Highest Purpose and Deepest Desires*

"The author takes leave of her east coast home and ailing husband to embark on an "inspired" adventure west. Along the way, she experiences various eye-opening and enlightening encounters which, woven together with flashbacks from her painful childhood, create for the reader a compassionate and often humorous memoir. I found the story to be a courageous testimony to second-half-of life soul work."

~ Vanessa Guerin,
Editor, *Radical Grace, Center for Action and Contemplation*

"Poignant, honest and laced with humor, Chris McMillan's memoir chronicles her journey, a search both literal and figurative, from her beginnings in hard-scrabble Georgia to marriage and adventure in far-flung lands. Woven through the stories of her past is the tale of her mid-life cross-country pilgrimage of self discovery. Caught on the cusp of the women's movement, McMillan questioned everything, accepted what was necessary, and grounded herself in a faith that transcended religion. Her irreverent reverence for life is indicative of her belief in self, and disbelief in a mandate of any kind. Inspirational without dogma, Backwards is a guide for anyone who has ever pondered the road not taken."

~ Marjorie Klein,
author of *Test Pattern*

"Chris McMillan is a pilgrim in the deepest sense of the word, a committed journeyer in pursuit of the sacred. By recounting the story of a two-month pilgrimage she undertook years ago in desperation for the survival of her soul, Chris's entire life is revealed as just such a committed quest. Her stories of deep interiority, along with keenly descriptive tales from a fascinating life, are raw and truthful, filled with insight, wit and pathos. A writer with this kind of courage for self-expression gives invitation to readers to find the same in themselves. This book is a very enriching read."

~ Tayria Ward,
author of *Depth Psychological Insights
Into Life and Dreams*, and *The Indigenous Mind.*

Backwards
off the Curb

BACKWARDS
OFF THE CURB

A Memoir

Chris McMillan

Continental Shelf Publishing
Savannah

sales@CSPBooks.com

Continental Shelf Publishing, LLC

4602 Sussex Place

Savannah, GA 31405

Cover design by Arlin Geyer,
Iris Photo & Digital Imagining

Library of Congress Control Number: 2011928387

McMillan, Christine

  Backwards Off the Curb

  ISBN 978-0-9831483-1-9 (alk. paper)

First Edition, July 2011

Printed in Canada

Dedication

I tell my story as an offering to all women, my sisters, who have, for whatever reason, found themselves hanging on the edge of madness until muscle developed so they could reach out and get a grip on sanity—no need to name them—they know who they are.

And to my granddaughter who read the first of my stories when she was fifteen years old and then said, "Gran, this has to be published."

And to all who laughed and cried with me in the appropriate places while I read to them. My thanks for "getting it" and for hoisting me up over the wall.

And to The Community Foundation of Western North Carolina, Women's Fund, who will benefit from a percentage of the proceeds from this book.

Preface

PATTERNS HAVE ALWAYS CAPTIVATED ME, quilts, oriental rugs, men's ties—I have gravitated to them as if drawn by an unseen force. My obsession with patterns began on the day my brother, Sammy, returned from World War II. He reached into his duffle bag and *poof,* three silk scarves magically appeared. The filmy pieces of fabric, treasures from a war zone, were like nothing I had ever seen. These scarves awakened me to a world beyond the shabby space my family called home. We existed in rooms filled with a hodgepodge of "get by" furnishings, the walls and floors were bare. Nothing there could be mistaken for art or good taste.

Sammy, small of stature, a shy, sandy-haired boy of eighteen, joined the infantry just days after he graduated from Savannah High. He became one of those "foot slogging" infantry guys who saw the worst of WWII in France and Germany. I was seven when he left and nine when he returned; horrors of war only registered with me as news reels at movie theaters, but my silky souvenirs were *for real,* they conjured no picture shows of war.

As I gazed at the shiny fabric, the vibrant jewel-toned colors must have created new connections in my juvenile brain. My stubby little finger traced the squiggly lines and found images hidden among the magenta, turquoise and plum strokes. These colors were not in the crayon boxes at 38th Street School. Swirls of bold black were interspersed, and caused figures to pop out and sway while I sat transfixed. The patterns became a magic carpet, my transportation out of the monotone drab existence I shared with my family in the house on Brady Street.

This memory has been the clearest recollection I've had from my early years. I call it my *transfigurative* moment. Three squares of fabric awakened me, and sent me on a search for color and contrast, for paths that twist and turn then end in a never-before-seen world.

I do not recall the day when the scarves vanished from my chest of treasures. Possibly they were discarded along with my Baby Magic Doll, whose rubbery life-like feel was designed to evoke the "mother instinct" in young girls of the 1940's—our highest and only calling. Also gone are the steamy letters from Jay Helmken and my Savannah High diploma, tossed out in some long ago purge of "junk." The letters, if they could be retrieved, might make me giggle and blush. The doll or the diploma would scarcely make an emotional dent, but those scarves, how I would love to touch them once again and wallow in their waves of color.

Without the actual scarves to caress, I have been forced to settle for an invisible wisp of memory. I've guarded this strand of silky filament and, in fact, hang on to it for dear life. It is from this thread that my story has been woven.

I hope that you, dear reader, will find here a precious strand of your own to help you spin your story. If I had a rope, I would toss it to you—for now, the strand will have to do.

Blessings on your journey,

Chris

Acknowledgments

THIS BOOK BEGAN WITH SCRIBBLINGS in a journal titled "Notes of a Mad Woman Gone Sane." From that messy, incoherent, rambling tangle of thoughts, a manuscript was birthed. Those who labored with me from conception to the final push are: Susan Snowden, Elizabeth McMillan, Sandra Smith, Allan Campo, Michael Mann, Lynne Diehl, Pamela Coble, Margaret Tichenor, Ruth Hill, Jan Davis, Jean Marie Luce, Anne Challen, Pam Lane, Anne Kimmel, Kelly McMillan and Fran Harris. Also my writing coach Jennifer Manlowe, my editor C.J. Dorgolah and my publicist Marji Young, all kept reminding me to breathe and to keep on pushing. Then to Lester who brought me wine every afternoon and eased the pain.

It's a book! I never would have made it without you— eternal gratitude to my team.

Leaving Home

AND WHEN YOU TURN TO THE RIGHT OR WHEN YOU TURN TO THE LEFT, YOUR EARS SHALL HEAR A WORD BEHIND YOU, SAYING, "THIS IS THE PATH, WALK IN IT."

ISAIAH 30:21

I RUSHED INTO THE GRAND old Peabody Hotel just in time to see the elevator doors slide open, and the ducks waddle out onto the red carpet that had been rolled out just for them. The royal waterfowl marched past their adoring subjects, me included, while the Duck Master in his red bell captain jacket led the way. Young boys, close by, giggled and punched each other. I felt envy; there was no one for me to giggle with or punch as I stood there in my jeans and sneakers, totally out of place with the other women in the crowd. The dress code appeared to be one of matched sweater sets and little flats with gold buckles, not Levis, sweatshirts and sneakers.

Missed that message—oh well. No one is looking at me anyway.

The Duck Parade had long been on my list of sights to see. I gravitate towards the absurd, and what could be more absurd than a bunch of ducks living like royalty in a hotel penthouse with their own master to watch over them? The ducks only do this ridiculous routine for three months and then they are put out to pasture in rural Tennessee. They are then replaced by a fresh gaggle that check into the hotel and then learn the daily drill.

The march ended when, with a little wing boost, each duck scaled the low wall surrounding the fountain, the splashy centerpiece of the lobby. There they set about to float peacefully. The parade happens in reverse in the afternoon when the troops flap their wings and land on the special red carpet to make the retreat to their luxurious quarters on the top floor—*what a life!*

Could this spectacle help me solve the mystery that has brought me out on the road, away from my home in search of god knows what? Why can't I be as special as those ducks? Where is the master who will guide me from my penthouse to the water where I can just float all day? My childhood fantasy of living in a magical land and wearing flowing robes while having maids draw my bath just ain't gonna' happen—get over it, Chris! You could fling yourself in the fountain and maybe the Master would escort you to the penthouse at the end of the day—or the loony bin.

I resisted the urge to jump in the water and float with the ducks; instead I chose to leave this peaceful setting of ducks drifting in meaningless circles. There were tourists dressed in mostly preppy attire sipping coffee at tables around the fountain. They looked as aimless as the ducks, as did I when crawling into the driver's seat of my dull gray van. I asked myself, "What next? Which direction should I take next?"

Last night I bedded down in Tupelo, Mississippi (the birthplace of Elvis) and, in the morning, I drove the short distance into Memphis all the while listening to Blue Grass on the radio. A song entitled "I Believe in What I Feel" gave me a mystical sense that I was on the right path (for now). Using my psychic, inner-navigation skills to find my way into the center of the city, I found the perfect parking place just across from the hotel.

Truth be told, I had no idea what I was feeling or why I happened to be in Memphis of all places, just around the corner from Beal Street, the home of the blues.

There's that color blue again. Am I here because I have a bad case of the blues?

God knows; I sure don't.

That night in Tupelo caused me to ponder, "Have I left home in order to chase after the ghost of Elvis?" That tacky motel room certainly bore his mark; there were no paintings on velvet, but he sure could have decorated it. I felt as though I might be in touch with the man who caused young women of my era to go into swoons of ecstasy.

There I was, fifty-four years old, a little past the midlife-crisis age. I wondered, "Can this really be the middle of my life? I don't want to live to be one-hundred-and-eight!" The truth was, I had no idea what I planned to do with the rest of my life and certainly had no idea of how long that might be. If I were depressed, would I have concocted this travel schedule with such attention to detail? I know I have a history of chasing my thoughts around in circles—kind of like those drifting ducks. Folks back home might say, "She just needs to get *aholt* of herself." Strange notions began to take over my conduct. The plan to run away came to me as though channeled by some disturbed spirit. I did not question the validity at the time; it made sense in some mysterious way. To others, it looked as though I had gone mad.

"Get out the maps, chart a course, get away and then figure out the next step. Just go and act like you know what you are doing. Fake it!" the spirit ordered. I had no doubt that this voice belonged to a wise woman with a hard-won experience of liberation. History shows us that what at first appears to be foolish can change the future forever. This *being* may have chained herself to a post outside the White House until women were given the right to vote.

I'm good at faking it—no problem. I can play any part I choose in this production. I could be Blanch DuBois from Streetcar Named Desire and live the rest of my life "relying on the kindness of strangers." Could wandering from town to town like a bona fide homeless person be any worse than this last year of mental torture has been in my so called cushy life in North Florida?

For the better part of 1990, I woke up each day in a deep dark pit, my work lacked meaning, my heart seemed to fade, and my spirit shrank a little more each day. I sold clothes to women who mostly had closets overflowing with last year's "must have" garments. My interest in flipping through magazines and analyzing the goofy get-ups of the so-called "trend setters" of the world had died. My strong competitive streak ran its last marathon; I no longer gave a damn about all the details of the life that I had previously thought relevant. I felt that my familiar creativity had flat-lined and that loud voice in my head—also familiar—would not let up. No matter how hard I tried to talk myself out of my hopeless thoughts, I just could not get back to the woman I'd known myself to be.

Mac, my witty, always-whistling-a-happy-tune husband and business partner, also looked as though he had lost the spark we used to share. He quit whistling and joking. His six-foot-four frame now slumped where previously he always stood with military erectness as though ready to lead his troops into battle.

I could only guess about his state of mind since he refused to talk about his condition. Like most men I knew, he rarely spoke of an inner life. But, at this time, he looked as though he had come unhinged, like a marionette soldier gone slack. "Our world" had come to a halt and now it was only "my world" and "his world." These worlds seemed separated by an invisible electric fence. We could find no space for the other in the dark holes into which we had fallen.

The difference between us, as I saw it, was that he had no one giving him "marching orders." The voice in my head shouted loud enough that it should have been heard on his side of the bed.

When I said goodbye in the kitchen on the morning of my leaving, we both cried. Still, I walked out without looking back. I focused with fierceness on the grey concrete and backed down our driveway. As I obeyed my own marching orders, I dried my eyes and hardened my heart.

Just go—do not look back—eyes straight ahead—it does not matter that you do not understand why—just go. So what if this place is filled with memories—just go. So you had the good life here— go. Your sanity depends on this—don't question— just go.

I headed west as the sun continued to rise in my rear view mirror. Goodbye Florida. Feeling like I was Thelma without Louise, I shouted, "Alabama and Mississippi here I come!"

The first night in that depressing motel, with my room right next to the office, I felt as though my body was no longer tethered to my mind and spirit—just a gauzy mass that the desk clerk would not see even if I ran outside naked. I missed my well-decorated home and could find no way to respond to the new nagging voice in my head that bullied me over and over, "Why in the hell are you here in this dump?" I had no answer except the same one a parent is often forced to give, "Because I say so." "Evasive answer," the nagger responded. The familiar reflection in the mirror gave me the only tangible evidence that I had actually chosen to position the sum total of me in this tacky room.

*Just remember, you did choose it. As they say, "There is no accounting for taste." Who the hell is **they** and what do **they** know about taste? Why should that matter to me now? Everything is changing.*

I hate television and my mind certainly could not focus on any reading material, so I analyzed the room's décor.

Are there schools of interior design for motels? Do trends change year to year? Why mauve and blue? Who makes a mattress that thin—why are there waves in it? Why are appearances so important to me?

Before plopping my single self on the double bed, I stored the gaudy bedspread in the corner. I hated touching that cheap, slinky fabric where surely body fluids from god-knows-who were embedded in the nylon fibers. Then I called Mac to report, "I've followed all your warnings as best I could. I've adhered to all the speed limits (not really) and my room is within hollering distance of the night clerk." Mac thought of those things that almost never crossed my mind. I humored him again by saying, "I parked the GM Safari van just outside the door; I'm safe and sound." I went on to say, "I'm planning to drive into Memphis to visit our old friends." This seemed to assure him though it was hard to know; he asked no questions, just acknowledged that he heard me. Mac had become a man of few words in the last year. He had that same deflated sound in his speech that I had been trying for months to confront. Each time I questioned him about his state of being, he came up with the same answer, "Leave me alone, I'm fine."

So, now I have left him alone, he's fine—sure!

I knew FINE *to be an acronym for "f…ing in need of everything."*

Months ago, I gave up making doctor appointments for him, because he would cancel them each time. I finally concluded that I had no ability to diagnose or treat his malady. He stubbornly refused to ask for help; I assumed he would figure it out in his own way and in his own time.

This crisis did not seem to be about our relationship, but what did I know? Trying to diagnose Mac caused my head to swim. Thoughts rolled through my head faster than I could follow them; it took all the focus I could muster just to hang on to the bar of this roller coaster that had become my mind. Family and friends would go whirling past in a blur. I could not hear the words they said, but I did catch the disapproving looks that told me they thought I had gone off my rocker.

Mama and my only sister, Frances (who like all oldest siblings felt responsible for everyone) expressed fear that divorce was in the offing. I had no balm to soothe their concerns; I couldn't make the fear vanish. Both of them loved Mac and I understood the dread they felt for both of us. At this time, I had plenty of doubt about the possibility of my return to marriage and living "happily ever after." This minefield that I was navigating put me outside my family's comfort zone and for sure near the edge of mine.

Mama also expressed her concern for my break with the Methodist Church—I expected no reconciliation there. My theology no longer conformed to that "old time religion." Neither of them could begin to comprehend my behavior of late. Fortunately, both Mama and Frances lived in Savannah, they were far enough away emotionally and geographically to play only bit parts in this particular scene in my seemingly lifelong play.

That morning, I had seen an ominous sign in northern Alabama, on my way to Tupelo. It said, "Go to Church or Burn Eternally." The words seem to float atop a background of flames. I did not intend to go back to church, so according to that prediction, I was headed straight for hell—*so be it.*

My friend Caroline has a saying that has always summed it up for me: "Most things are not a matter of right or wrong, it's just that some things are more fun than others." Both in my past and in my present, I choose fun every time with full awareness that my idea of fun could feel like *sinfulness* to another. However, I saw the rationale for this "all alone" journey as a deadly serious one. But giving it a name or defining the mission, I could not.

I thought, "I may be headed for hell, but the flames I expect to consume me will be those of passion, not of perdition." I had no doubt that my aimless plan came out of a burning desire for meaning, not out of questioning the rightness or wrongness of anything about my present actions. I would leave that judgment to others and I suspected the line of jurors had started to form.

My trial has begun.

If questioned, I would assure them that I did not intend to be on Monty Python's search for The Holy Grail. Even though my next stop was to be a convent in Kentucky, the "call" to the convent left me shaking my head in disbelief.

This journey must have the look of a scavenger hunt for the absurd. The thought of a week of silence and contemplation feels as bizarre as a bunch of ducks living in a penthouse. Will the nuns think I am a total fool? I do not know what to tell them if they want to know why I landed on their doorsteps.

Mama often said with great pride, "Well, I certainly was not going to ask any questions." I had always felt this adage took points off her IQ score. Not asking questions seemed sort of stupid. My recent inability to question these getaway plans gave me pause: "Do I have more in common with Mama than I could ever admit?"

The thought of Mama and my family led me to the awareness that all that family history tagged along, invited or not. I could not escape the shame and pain nor the joys and accomplishments of the past just by packing my boots, journals and jeans in a van. Fifty-four years could not be blotted from memory. The ghosts of the past eternally follow and haunt—at least, mine do.

Who invited you to get into this van? Damn it! I thought I left you back in Quincy.

Can You Spell Atmosphere?

*LIFE CAN ONLY BE UNDERSTOOD BACKWARDS, BUT WE
MUST LIVE IT FORWARD.*

KIERKEGAARD

MAMA NEVER CARED MUCH FOR facts; she preferred her own version of reality. The decision to spell her name "M-a-y-m-e" instead of "M-a-m-i-e," as her birth certificate read, appears to be the first evidence that she altered truth to suit her whim. This metamorphosis happened in 1917 when Mamie Frances Boyd, a sixteen-year-old sophomore in a South Georgia boarding school, dreamily confessed the new identity to her classmates.

"The spelling of my name doesn't suit me. I think a name with a 'Y' in it is more impressive. I can perfectly picture how it will look in the paper when my engagement is announced," she said in her most theatrical voice. Obviously Mama had an image of her dream guy, even though no visible suitor appeared on her horizon. Mayme must have schemed, dreamed and conjured daily incantations to turn her phantom into flesh and blood.

Three years later, enter Sam—tall, dark and handsome. Mama met him when she rode the train on the weekends from her school in Douglas, Georgia. Sam worked in the depot of her hometown, West Green. Sam did not come from the Landed Gentry, no pedigree, unlike Mama's family who saw themselves as a "cut above" many of their dirt-poor neighbors in this little piney woods corner of Georgia. Sam not only lacked education, he also came up short on ambition. He daydreamed about the possibility of a life as a professional baseball player, the same way Mayme daydreamed of being rescued by a Prince. Mama did not know a lick about baseball—could not tell a curve ball from a slider. Prince Sam with his tall thin, athletic, sexy body captured little Mayme at first glance. She couldn't resist his skill for (bullshit) chatter in their train depot *tête-à-têtes*—the topper must have been his amazing ability to communicate in Morse code.

I picture Mayme getting off the train in West Green wearing her middy blouse, pleated skirt, and silk stockings, the boarding-school fashion of the day. She would cast her eyes towards the little station, where Sam was tapping out messages with one hand and waving to her with the other. This world surely looked like one embedded with secret codes and ethereal wonders. Mayme was helpless to resist his allure.

Some insight into Mama's worldview came to me years later while we were having lunch in the ornate dining room of The Hershey Hotel. While we looked out on to the perfectly designed, blossoming garden of this grand old establishment, Mama, in her eighties at that time, gazed across the table and said, "I just love *atmosphere*." The dreamy look on her face said it all. I saw then how her life had been a quest for some special setting that helped match her inner vision of life to the outer world. My only response was to flash her one of my smart-ass, all-knowing looks.

For my entire life, this woman had decorated our home with cheap knick knacks in a constant effort to create *atmosphere*, alright—one that never succeeded to hide the fact of poverty. Mayme's logic about buying useless *pretties* came from the same logic she used about changing the spelling of her name. Her salt and pepper shaker collection, her crocheted toilet paper covers, and dime store figurines impressed no one, as far as I could see. Tacky trinkets surely looked different through Mayme's eyes than they did through mine.

Mayme must have been quite impressed to see her engagement to John Samuel Young appear in the *Coffee County News*, especially considering that each of them had a "Y" in their name. The newspaper's use of flowery language matched Mama's gift for illusion, turning Sam's job as a telegraph operator into an impressive position with The G & F Railroad. The announcement could lead one to believe Mayme had snagged a winner, or at least an up-and-coming type.

"Miss Mayme's driving her ducks to a poor pond," according to "Uncle Mose," the hired man who was probably called "boy" by the elders in the family. Mose had known Mayme for her whole life so he knew her silliness. One generation free from slavery, he lived in the little house behind their big house, which was not exactly a plantation, but certainly gave the message that Mayme's people were "folks of substance."

Mama thought Mose's warning about her impending marriage was ridiculous. I heard the story often; she seemed to think it quaint and entertaining. Mama would have done well to heed Mose's wisdom. Too bad Mayme refused to take seriously his foreboding prediction. To my mind, he was a prophet worthy of respect.

Still, Mayme held tightly to her image as the cute little daughter of the prosperous lumberman and, like most young folks, the thought never crossed her mind that she could lose this exalted position. Mayme assumed that "the way it had been would be the way it would always be." Her younger and only sibling, Ethel, also wore the latest fashions, went to an exclusive school and, as I heard them tell the story often, had the finest buggy in town. As long as they could hold onto it, the entire family clung to their class position.

In any event, history would show that Mayme, indeed, had made a poor choice; Sam did not provide her with the style of living to which she had become accustomed. Sam, in fact, had no buggy and, though automobiles soon became plentiful, he navigated the world afoot until much later in his life.

One marriage and three babies later, with the country spiraling into financial despair, Mayme "with a *Y*" sank into her own Great Depression. Frances, the firstborn, came along nine months after Mama's wedding day, followed by Sammy and Harold ("Hap") at three-year intervals. I, her fourth and last child, accidentally came nine years later. These "little burdens" surely were far more than Mayme had envisioned when she charted this course. The ordinariness of "real life" definitely did not match the fantasies created in Mama's boarding school dorm. Her fragile constitution could not handle the disappointment. She crumbled like an over-baked cornbread.

My best guess is that bit by bit and baby by baby, her world fragmented like shards of a broken mirror. The "bad luck" came, as it is wont to do, with a predictable dreariness. Mama was never inclined to perform domestic chores like cooking and housekeeping, add diapers, sleeplessness and the unrelenting wailng of needy babies; she simply came *unspooled.* "A case of the vapors" was an acceptable diagnosis for her time.

When her Daddy died in the early 1930's, she pocketed her small inheritance, and left her three young'uns to be cared for by her own Mama. Then she promptly plopped herself down in North Carolina's famous sanatorium in Southern Pines. This was a time when many wealthy Yankees traveled south to "take the cure." It seemed to be the perfect answer for Mama who surely loved hanging out with rich folks, even if they were funny talking northerners. Add a night now and then with daddy, her lover, and you've got *atmosphere.*

Back in West Green, Mayme's doctor told her that she might have contracted tuberculosis, the dreaded disease of the day. Even the remote possibility gave Mama all the permission she needed to get the hell away from those tedious domestic responsibilities. She confessed in later years that she was quite sure she never had that *awful* disease, but that awareness did not stop her from spending her whole inheritance at the sanatorium/health spa on the iffy diagnosis.

In her final years, Mama would reminisce about her time in a rocking chair on the front porch in Southern Pines. I picture "Miss Mayme" in the bucolic setting with not a care in the world—ah, what peace. With great pride she recounted how cleverly she could deceive the nurses and attendants: "I'd spit the medicine out when the nurse left the room. I hated milk and would pour it in the potted plant next to the dining table," she bragged. She saw her time there as a vacation and certainly nothing to do with becoming disease free.

As far as I could tell, it never crossed Mayme's mind to use her father's money, approximately five thousand dollars, differently; maybe give the family a little pampering—like food in the pantry. A traditional homemaker's practical thoughts would not find any place in Mayme's consciousness. Even though I was not yet born, hearing this story still amps up my rage level to maximum decibels. If she was sick, why in the hell did she not take the meds and drink the damn milk? Too, if she was not sick, why was she allowed to take a bed away from a Tubercular patient in need during a global pandemic?

Still, I have found myself face-to-face with my own habits of running away. Such behaviors continue to piss me off when I observe them under *that* same microscope! Am I really that different from Mama? She went to Southern Pines to escape a traditional wife's lot. I fled west.

Because the family did without to finance her outrageous sense of luxurious entitlement, I cannot resist judging her unfit. But, if I dig a little deeper, I'd be forced to see the implications for my loved ones regarding my own inner-mandate to flee the family scene and go galloping off in search of *my peace.*

Like Scarlet O'Hara, "I'll just think about that tomorrow."

***** *

Once satisfied that I had seen enough of the regal ducks and The Peabody Hotel, I navigated my way to the eastside of Memphis and found the home of our friends, neighbors from our Omaha days at Offutt Air Force Base, Carlo and Sally Ann. After a warm greeting, we did the usual check-in: first, how successful our kids had become, and then the "one-up" routine about our precious grandchildren. I had only one, so they beat me on numbers; after all they were Catholics, at least they were twenty-three years ago, when we were neighbors.

After the catch up period, they began to quiz me about the purpose of this trip. "Why are you running away? What does

Mac have to say about this separation?" Then the inquisition began about my politics. They remembered when I shifted my point of view in the late 1960's when we all lived on the base. I became one of the egregious labels of the day: "those liberals," "a pinko," or worse. Their puzzled faces bespoke judgment as I tried to explain myself. I gave it my best shot to make sense of my political position. "I am sick of my country's cavalier ways about war. Under George H. Bush, the country seems to have degenerated into a bunch of flag worshippers and I refuse to make the red, white and blue into my god." I know this not only baffled them, it pushed them over the edge. Surely, they saw me as a totally lost soul. My words did nothing for my case—the gavel came down—"guilty as a traitor."

They shifted the subject and began to tell about how they had left the Catholic Church. They now worshiped in one of those mega-churches, with giant screens that flash the words to "praise songs" while the congregation, with raised hands, swayed to the music. Overcome by the spirit, they were swept up in this charismatic, ecstasy stuff. I was astounded that Carlo—a New Yorker, first generation Italian, and educated Air Force pilot—could join in such a cultist form of religious expression. For Sally Ann, raised in rural Georgia, traveling around to tent revival meetings with a family who sang Gospel music, the conversion downward made more sense. Those two had always been an odd match.

A favorite saying of Gran's seemed to be just right for the situation, "To each his own, said the old woman as she kissed the pig." One thing I knew for sure: I did not plan to kiss their pig. Their form of anesthetizing religious fervor had no appeal to me.

Before long, they revealed their true agenda: "The devil is obviously tempting you and, without intervention, he will win the battle for your soul." They wanted to make an appointment for me to talk with their pastor. Because I truly loved this couple and felt they honestly cared for me, I decided to submit to their request even though I knew there was no chance that I could be 'won over' to their point of view.

Clearly, I was an emergency case. The next day I walked into the enormous church building, found the office and told the receptionist that I had an appointment with "Pastor Bob"—I did not even have his last name. He was promptly summoned and came out with a "Hail fellow well met," pompous smile on his face. I knew the type and I knew the cadence of his speech before the first words came out; I could hear the sermon coming. I braced myself, and dutifully followed him into his office. The door closed and the smile vanished as soon as he placed his portly body down into his throne tucked behind his immense desk. The look then became one of distress. He peered over the top of his reading glasses and looked down at me as if pushing me under the righteousness of his gaze. Relenting, I slumped in my smaller chair. I put on my most serious "big girl" face and kept telling myself, "Do not laugh." I could hear Mama saying, "He is the preacher, you be nice!"

The flames began to gather around me as he started his lecture. He knew why my friends were concerned for my soul. "There are some places we can go that it then becomes impossible to find our way back to GOD. We are the ones who put ourselves out of reach, but GOD is always available! We must be careful about the choices that take us to that *place of no return*," he sternly preached. With eyes blazing straight through me, his one-person congregation, I knew for certain that I would not become another sheep of his boundless flock.

I fanned myself and thought about asking him my "passion or perdition" question. I knew instantly that if I did use the word passion, he would translate it to mean sex and then everyone's worst fears would be confirmed. This trip would seem to be about me having a lover, an illicit rendezvous. I restrained myself and only listened.

Pastor Bob warned me: "If you turn your back on this opportunity to be saved, the devil could claim you for eternity!" Listening to his seemingly endless fears felt like truer flames of eternity. I fanned myself a little more.

Why in the hell did I agree to this meeting? Who is it helping?—not me! Get me out of here. Judgment about the other is bouncing around in here like a tennis match.

My eyes must have signaled to him that I had checked out, like those folks in church who look at their watches and tap them to make sure they haven't stopped. Many of his parishioners must stare vacantly at him, a verbose minister and salesman, still, he droned on past the noon hour with his incessant brand of "The Good News." At that point, he got it. He realized his defeat. All he could do was to pray over me from his taller throne and then release me to the flames. The FATHER GOD part boomed out like long trapped gas. Finally, the "AMEN" came. I have blotted out the words of that awful, condemning prayer. I only know it dragged on and on, interminable and excruciating. After that AMEN, I sprang from the chair, thanked him for his concern, sprinted to my nice cool, air-conditioned van and set the control on max-high. Suddenly, I heard my next directive, "Get the *hell* out of Memphis!" I did.

To say I became lost to my old friends would be a gross understatement. Christmas cards and letters soon ceased and our paths did not cross again. Mac probably became the focus of their prayers, since they saw him as the victim of my irredeemable madness. I crossed the state line into Kentucky with my sense of freedom restored. In Bardstown, I checked into another nondescript motel, Wayside Rest Inn—again, choosing the room right next to the office. I began getting my head together for the next day's check-in to the convent. No one I had ever known had spent a week in a convent—I had no guides. Silence and contemplation did not even get honorable mention in my Protestant world. We measured spirituality by the list of good deeds done.

Contemplation in "southern speak" translated into, "I'm fix'n to do something." One might say, "I'm contemplating what I'm gonna' cook for dinner." I spoke "southern," and only god knew the language of the convent. Fear consumed me. Awareness that I would look foolish to these authentic Holy Women seemed to expand even while I slept. An even larger bogeyman came in the form of images of a psychotic episode. I could see my body being dragged away in restraints by attendants from the asylum. The horror show flashed off-and-on through the night and right into my morning coffee time.

God, please don't let me make a total fool of myself. I know I am acting crazy and you certainly know it, but couldn't we just make it 'our little secret'?

God gave me no clue that my pleading prayer might be worthy of granting. There were no guarantees, especially not for this skeptic. Peace did not come and I received no assurance about any Convent Survival Skills. I would have to just suck it up and take the leap.

I needed a little time to adjust and orient myself before laying my pathetic body down on the convent altar. After motel check-out, I acted like a tourist and browsed around as though I had come to see how bourbon, the major industry of the area, found its way into bottles and liquor stores. The vapors of the strong spirits, stored in huge vats, permeated the air. I had no serious attraction to those spirits or their origins, instead my eyes feasted on the scenes of a simple lifestyle, the quaint village and beautiful farmland. Allowing my focus to rest on the landscape brought my first measure of peace since leaving home.

"You must be from out of town," the waitress in Ye Olde Pub asked as I pondered the lunch menu. I could have told her I was from *way* out of town—and for sure I was out of my league. Or maybe I had no league at all—just simply a lost soul looking for home. Instead I merely replied, "I'm from Florida."

"I sure would like to go down there one day and take my kids to Disney World," she said longingly.

"Yes, that is a good place to take the kids." I failed to mention that I had, *with great pride*, never set foot on Disney soil in Florida.

Why could I not have such a clearly-defined goal as this young woman? A trip to Disneyland or the Grand Canyon, those are enough for 'normal' people. They do not go chasing around to places where they have no idea why they came: a sighting of Mickey Mouse could be enough—why not me?

Kentucky orientation completed, I proceeded on to Loretto in the tiny community of Nerinx. As I entered the grounds, my tape player intoned *Pachelbel's Canon*. I traveled in the same state, this was an entirely different world. I drove past a large pond encircled with walking paths, rolling hills of manicured green space, plum and pear trees soon to bud out. In the background, I could see several multi-storied, red brick buildings with white trim—definitely the turn-of-the-century style. I felt "at home" and "at peace," despite lingering doubts about the temporariness of both experiences during what I was sure would be a long week. The verdant scene overwhelmed me, took my breath away—I had to pull to the side of the road and let my hovering spirit come back into my body. And yet, even in sublime moments such as these, there was Mac-the-ghost, lurking expressionless in the corner of my awareness. Since the day I had left him with tears on his cheeks, I had called home at the same time each day for my obligatory check-in. Every conversation confirmed my feeling that he was slipping through my fingers, still, I had no idea what was behind it. He had begun to look old, his stooped walk and mask-like facial expression haunted me. My handsome and worldly lover had, like Elvis, "left the building." A freight train of grief rode beside me in the van, along with loneliness and some measure of fear. Like a disgruntled soul being dragged into the next realm, Mac's pallid image never left me. Feelings of betwixt and between commitments relentlessly accompanied me into my "silent" retreat.

At the same time, I knew I was not equipped to fix or enliven Mac. I left that job to god—whatever that meant. God had become just a little speck somewhere in my interior, not a big G that sat on a throne "up there." Whatever Mac did or did not do had little to do with this quest of mine. I needed repairs—this crisis of meaning belonged to me alone. My job was to come to terms with my uncertain life and let go of all my tired and tightly held illusions of love, a predictable future, or the longed-for comforts of security.

Maybe I will have to kiss a pig, after all.

Brady Street

BECAUSE THINGS ARE THE WAY THEY ARE, THINGS WILL NOT STAY THE WAY THEY ARE.

BERTOLD BRECHT

I CAME INTO THE WORLD in Stilson, Georgia where Daddy, along with his father, found temporary work in the turpentine business. Just before this time, Daddy moved up to Ohio where he had followed the rails until that income source dried up. Like so many workers, he returned to Georgia in utter defeat. Of course, Mayme's inheritance only existed as a warm memory in her head. The six of us were packed like smelly sardines into a little tenant house out in the back woods of Bullock County where poverty and pine trees abounded. My brothers, then ages eight and eleven, could never recall the day that I popped out and into their lives. My sister, who was fourteen at my birth, had perfect recollection, and still does even to this day.

> *How could the birth of a baby, right there in the house, not leave a lifelong imprint in memory? Ho-hum there's a baby in the house—where did she come from?*

When I was three years old, my Granddaddy died and Daddy finally found a real job in Savannah. He went to work for National Gypsum on the Savannah River. In 1940, the family, which now included Gran (Daddy's mama), moved into a house on Brady Street that was owned by Calvary Baptist Church. We rented it for fifteen dollars a month. The house showed no sign of ever having had a coat of paint and looked as depressed as my Mama, who seldom ventured out the front door.

Mama must have suffered from agoraphobia—a word we certainly had never heard spoken. A diagnosis for my form of anguish would have been quite the opposite. I wanted to get the hell out of that house, the only choice available was to perch on the front steps and watch the happenings in the neighborhood. Mama looked sad and frightened most of the time. Living in the big city of Savannah must have caused her to fall into that black pit once again. This time she had no money to go running off to a sanatorium for rest and recuperation. It was as if the front door had a bolt on it, when in fact there was not a lock at all. She holed up in the house, preferring to keep herself "locked in" and safe from the outer world.

At age forty, gum disease claimed Mama's teeth; during the weeks before the dentures went in, she was a frightening sight. Mayme Frances, the belle of West Green became the frump of Savannah, with her caved in mouth, teary eyes and *uncoiffed* quill like hair. She moped around in a worn out cotton dress that hung limp from her slight frame. These images, to this day, are fixed with great detail in my memory.

My first journey to the "dark side of life"—a deep melancholy—began this same year, in 1941. I traveled there often in years to come and most often encountered "the witch" who sort of looked like Mama. Psychologists say that the earliest experiences play a major role in shaping who one will become. Certainly, my formative memory is one of despair regarding Mama's condition. One picture that I often replay is of the four-year-old me sitting helpless in the dilapidated garage behind the house and allowing the grime there to soak into my pores. The mold formed me just as much as that dank garage matched my mood. I wanted the spiders and creepy crawly bugs there to take me with them into their more hospitable lairs. Mostly, I wanted the magic wand that could transform Mama into the Queen of her fantasies, which was surely hidden behind her armor of a deadening depression. No such wand appeared. Neglect for herself and the rest of us seemed to rule all of our days.

Roaches were always visible in this truly nasty house, but in the dark of night, they came out in platoons. The moment a light went on in the kitchen, we'd hear them scurrying for cover like thieves in the night. The precise sound is easy for me to replay in my mind and anyone who has ever heard this knows exactly what I mean—a perfect background for a horror movie.

Our kitchen appliances consisted of one each of the following: a kerosene stove, a 1930's ice box (the kind that holds a block of ice) and a single window that served as the garbage disposal. Mama simply tossed all coffee grounds and food scraps right out into our "backyard." This slimy spot in the dirt oozed next to the rickety wooden steps that came down from the second floor where Mrs. Jones and her two creepy teenage sons lived. Those boys always had a greasy look about them. They were as repugnant to me as the roaches scuttling around our kitchen.

It seems that the kitchen window was never closed. I suspect it served as an escape for the kerosene fumes emitted by the stove, though it was the tension between Mama and

Gran working together in that dinky space that was toxic enough to kill us all. Mama would walk to that window and fling out the scraps with a look of vengeance. Daddy did the ranting and cussing, but Mayme dealt with the family "refuse" in a far more subtle way: hurling scraps and leftovers out the window spoke volumes without uttering one word.

Why does Mama never say what she is thinking? I can hear her, but she does not say the words out loud.

Because Mama dreaded leaving the house, she often sent me to the store to pick up needed items. One day, she hollered out into the yard for me to come and do her bidding at the little neighborhood corner market. I took the empty milk bottle from the kitchen and the loose change from her hand and skipped off in my usual barefooted manner. Full bottle in hand, I began the return trip when, suddenly, I stubbed my toe and crashed to the sidewalk. My left arm landed solidly on top of a jagged piece of glass and I knew, right then, that this cut would require more than we had in our homemade first-aid kit. Kerosene on the open wound, and then a clean rag tied around it could not repair this gaping wound.

Oh no, Mama will have to leave the house. I have done an awful thing—it's all my fault.

I can still see the look of absolute horror on her face when I came screaming in the back door with blood spurting from my arm, gushing out on to the linoleum floor. She grabbed a rag, held it around my arm and dragged me out as she yelled for the one neighbor, Mrs. Lanier, who had a car. They rushed my bloody body to Candler Hospital, just across from the big park where I loved to play with my Brady Street friends. I had seen the big building lots of times, but had never walked through the doors. Mama in her bloody dress and me with a huge blood-soaked rag around my arm had the nurse/

nuns flocking to us as quickly as we became visible in their emergency room.

When a doctor appeared after the wound was cleaned, he said clamps had to be used to hold the crescent-shaped gash together. My tender skin could not take the stitches. Who would have ever believed any part of me was tender. I thought of myself as tough. When the hospital finished with me, Mama and I rode the bus home.

Poor Mama, out in public with a bloody child beside her—this is humiliating. Why did Mrs. Lanier not wait and drive us home? I hate that I have caused this embarrassment.

Today, I look at the scar on my left arm just above my wrist and still feel the pain of that child who believed she was responsible for her Mama's depression, a girl with such awareness of her family's poverty that the cost of a broken bottle and spilled milk registered more than physical pain and loss of blood. No one directly imposed the excessive weight of responsibility that I had struggled under as a child. But, on the day that bottle broke, the seven-year-old me could not see the martyr role as just one role among many that I learned to play. The pattern must have been embedded in my being—it felt natural.

Mama's milk and my blood swirling together must have made a spooky picture on the sidewalk that was just a few yards from our house. I would like to capture it on canvas, but details of that pattern seem to be too fragile in my mental storehouse. Maybe one day it will come into greater focus. It causes me to ponder the questions, "Did Mama nurse me?" "Did I ever suck from her breasts?" I doubt it. Any happening where body awareness should come into play, Mama always went missing. When I hit the teen years, I had to use my babysitting money for sanitary napkins and bras. Mama never let on that her baby child might have such a need. My sister later told me that she also had to fend for herself when she came of age.

I knew, without a doubt, that my birth into this family had caused Mama's depression. I carried the burden for my entire childhood. I thought I had barged in to rob them of a more gracious, genteel life—one I was certain they had before the time in Stilson. Now, because of my birth, all they could afford was this Brady Street existence of squalor. Often I imagined how it must have looked when the family played games in the parlor of Granddaddy Boyd's house in West Green. The cook would bring in lemonade on a little silver tray and Mose would work serenely in the garden as he sang gospel music. No one ever told me about that life; the lush details were mine alone.

That sort of thinking always led to more fantastic thoughts that I would never share with anyone. I wondered if a *me* even existed before January 4, 1937. Did I lurk in the bushes in my invisible, filmy, unborn body and spy on these people who would one day become my family? I have a strange, out-of-body awareness that haunts some version of the *real me*, the one born that day in Stilson. I have no idea how such a notion got planted, yet it has always lingered. This parallel world almost comes into view, even today, and it feels as though I stumble into that place before I catch myself and do a little side step.

Mayme found her fantasy "fix" by listening to the 1940's radio soap operas. They gave her the escape she clearly craved from our mangy existence and certainly respite from her miserable mother-in-law and their ongoing war. *Portia Faces Life* transported Mama to another world. Perhaps she let herself feel Portia's problems as a means to avoid her own;

I could hear her moan, "Oh no!" when poor Portia had one among her many dreadful experiences in her never-ending search for happiness as the wife of Lord Somebody. Or maybe it was *Our Gal Sunday* who married Lord Somebody—memory fades about such interchangeable characters.

Another means of escape for Mama seemed to come when the Jewel T man, a door-to-door salesman, appeared for the weekly visit. Mama poured over the pages of his catalog, each one filled with treasures for the home. She would then hand over a dollar for her weekly payment and maybe some odd change from the little coin purse in her apron pocket. She completed the transaction by submitting the much marked-out and scribbled over order for next week's delivery. The matched set of "special" dishes with little orange and brown stylized petals were the first of her purchases. Each week, she added to the collection until, finally, we owned even the iced tea pitcher in this not-so-special-to-my-eye pattern.

Soon she branched out to sources other than Jewel T, procuring a twelve-person service of silver-plated flatware, followed by a Duncan Phyfe mahogany dining table and sideboard.

Our house had no hot water, refrigerator, or central heat. Wallpaper was completely missing in many places and flapped like flimsy flags in others. Not one of us seemed to be able to claim ownership of any private space in this house. There were three rooms with beds, but I never heard anyone say that one was their very own bedroom. To this day, Frances and I cannot remember who slept where. This fuzziness of sleeping space is just one more childhood "memory" I have filed in my mystery folder.

We burned coal in a fireplace and took baths in an enamel washbasin in front of the fire. The iceman delivered on days we had money to pay him and clothes were washed on a scrub board in the bathtub and hung outside to dry. Still Mama was determined to create an "atmosphere" of "old money," by god! Albeit, on the installment plan.

Thanksgiving dinner, 1946, Mama served us multiple courses starting with Campbell's Cream of Tomato Soup in the Jewel T soup bowls along with the silver soup spoons. Mild fall weather kept us from the realization that there existed no heat source in the room. The Campbell's soup warmed us for a while. A baked hen, cornbread dressing, green peas with jellied cranberry sauce, slithering out from a can, came next. The final course and *pièce de résistance* was chocolate pudding from a mix with egg whites swirled through making it light and fluffy, Mama's version of "floating island."

Mayme was in high cotton, serving this festive meal as we sat at the elegant Duncan Phyfe table. Without a doubt, we had the holiday spirit—the way they do in those big houses on Victory Drive.

Daddy sucked down his own holiday spirits from the bottle he kept stashed in the hiding place *du jour*. At intervals throughout the meal, he would mumble something, disappear momentarily, and then return obviously well-fortified for his unintelligible and seemingly endless tirade. Daddy thought he could keep the visible source of his drinking out of sight, but the fact that he was drunk was undeniable. The more times he left the table, the louder, more vulgar and obnoxious he behaved on the return. His crude language embarrassed me. I heard the "F" word long before it came into vogue as an everyday, common word.

Drinking, swearing, and poverty formed a three-part centerpiece for our home. Daddy had the power, and though he was never physically abusive, his behavior left me with a feeling of being battered. I blamed him for all the ills of the household and believed he held the key to my cage. I longed for liberation and yet, at that time, could achieve it only through my imagination.

Surely these folks are not my real family—must be a mistake—we look absurd sitting around our fine antique replica mahogany table—who the hell are they? How did I get tangled up in this mess? The stork must have dropped me on the wrong steps.

My escape often came in the form of an invitation to spend the night with my best friend, Carolyn, who had the luxury of hot water, bubble baths, chintz floral bedspreads and starched, ironed pillowcases. The Smiths lived just around the corner, but it might as well have been another planet. Naturally, I never invited Carolyn to spend the night with me. The inner sanctum of Brady Street trashiness could not be viewed by outsiders.

My two brothers worked as newspaper or telegraph delivery boys. They also cut and sold kindling that was held together in bundles by rubber bands cut from tire inner tubes. Frances went to work downtown at Kress Ten Cent Store. Some of her meager wages went to buy me the most beautiful dress I had ever owned. It was made of burgundy velvet with little pearl buttons and had lace around the collar. A picture of me in it hangs on my wall today and reminds me, daily, of the possibility of having something luxurious in the worst of times.

Then the big war happened and all sorts of things began to change. My brother Sam, at age 18, signed up for the army right out of high school. Hap then quit school, at age 16, to work at the plant with Daddy. Our Brady Street gang played war with guns made from sticks and clothespins. Inner-tube strips, like the boys used for their kindling business, became ammunition for our guns. These rubber missiles left welts and taught us that war leaves its mark and, possibly, a lasting scar.

Families put small signs in their front windows displaying a star for each loved one serving in the military. Ours had only the one star for Sammy. Many houses in the neighborhood had stars in the window, but others, according to Daddy, "weaseled out of *the call*." Daddy could easily slip into one of his liquor-induced rants about the "Sorry son-of-a-bitch cowards!" His voice rose with disdain as he continued his rage-filled cussing.

There were citywide blackouts: a siren would sound and all the lights in the house would go out. *Inner Sanctum* or *Amos and Andy* on the radio kept us company as we huddled in the dark. During one of these drills, I remember sitting by the fire while Hap taught me to tie my shoes. Except for radio programs and these bizarrely mundane life skill lessons, those were frightening times. War and darkness merged together and left its black pattern permanently charred in my mind.

My memory of the day the war ended is vague, but the day FDR died is clearly etched there by my Mama's reaction. She wailed when she heard the news; she already looked sad most of the time, but to see her cry with wracking sobs made no sense to me.

Why is she crying? She didn't even know him. Who was this man and what did he have to do with us?

The family never explained, so I just watched and formed my own answers to my questions. I barely understood what it meant to be the President and certainly nothing about his bearing on our family. I knew not one person who had answers.

For some unknown reason, a shift happened. I associate this time of Mayme's deep grief with a drastic change in her demeanor. I have no clue who found the magic wand; I only know the sleeping princess awoke. She bought new clothes and not only went out the front door, but stayed for frightfully long periods. Her new dentures were in place at last and her body appeared to have a more solid form. Mayme was resurrected.

Women's groups, like The Daughters of Rebecca, The Pythian Sisters and Eastern Star, became the focus of her life. These secret sisterhoods, for Mama, were heaven-sent; she finally found her place in the world. I would lie in bed each night, waiting to hear her return, unable to imagine where she had been for such a long time. My mind would jump from one question to the next, things I would never ask her.

What do those ladies do at these meetings? What is the secret code they use to open the door? Do they use some of those cuss words I know? Probably not— ladies don't do that, just Daddy. Is she ever coming home? It's late and I'm scared. I wish I knew their password—damn it!

Sometimes these women even wore matching taffeta dresses. That alone would have been enough for me to know I would never join this or any such organization. Even at the age of nine, I understood tacky—the matching dresses most often came in pastel shades—ugh.

When our phone rang, Mama would get a pained look on her face, as though she had an unpleasant task facing her. Mayme's best acting skills came forth with the grimacing act; we knew this was the highlight of her day, since most likely her "sisters," Grace or Maggie, would be on the other end. Most of the airtime in this *tête-à-tête* concerned a certain club member and her non-compliant ways. Mama would roll her eyes, let out a sigh, stiffen up and say, "Well, after all, there are rules and she knows it and we all know it." Then she would soften with the final pronouncement: "Bless her heart, I love her to death, but she just has to stop acting so uppity—it's just not right."

The unspeakable, unnamable acts committed by the wayward sister would require long telephone autopsies by Mama, Grace, and Maggie, and were often punctuated with, "Well I never!" or "I swan!" both southernisms for "I swear"—ladies just cannot swear. "Have you ever *heard* of such a thing?" Mama would exclaim (it wasn't a question).

Each conversation also included at least some bit of negative analysis about the one who was not on the line at the time: "Well, you know, Maggie," Mama would say with her most authoritative voice, "I think Grace just likes to bellyache. The doctor has told her he can't find a thing wrong."

On the flip side, Grace, who had no children, loved to analyze Maggie's mothering skills. Maggie had an only child, Jesse, a boy one year older than me. She ruled both son and husband with an iron fist. "Henpecked," Mama and Grace agreed.

"When Maggie *blares* her eyes, Jesse and Rufus jump up and do whatever she tells them." I had never heard the word *blare* used to describe eyes but, to Mama, it fit the way Maggie took control of folks. The look must have made a harsh sound in Mama's mind.

"Maggie sews lace on Jesse's underwear," Mama would speak assuredly, knowing that her judgment was understood. A domineering mother would often be considered to be the cause of Jesse's little swish and feminine type gestures. Such code is something Mama could speak well; the language of the forties did not include the word "gay" except as a reference to the mood of a festive party.

In spite of "those ways," Jesse became a very successful international businessman living in his own apartment on Park Avenue. He'd always leave a key for me when I was in town and, during my visits, we would spend hours reliving our young lives in Savannah, sharing stories of our mothers and how they thrived on their "memberships" in secret societies. No proof of the "lace on his underwear" ever surfaced. He did lose all traces of his Georgia lower-middle-class background; he spoke Yankee very convincingly. Jesse died much too young—damn cigarettes. I still miss him. He validated my memories of our Mamas and their enthusiasm for passwords, initiations, and matching dresses.

Mama could never end her telephone conversations with a simple closing such as, "nice talking with you, need to go." No, Mayme had to insert a little drama. Every conversation ended with the same skit: she would quietly knock on the wall above the telephone and say, "There is someone at the door." This game must have amused her friends because, as far as I know, they never confronted her about her little charade. For Mama, making up a story was always much more fun than speaking some banal truth.

True, I had no appreciation for Mama's gift for creating reality. Little did I realize that I had my own version of "make believe." I would decorate our home over and over in my mind. Each day I changed the color of the walls and rearranged the furniture. Not furniture we *actually* had, but the furniture I could conjure up in my mind. Out of thin air, art would appear. Flowers grew up out of the hard-packed dirt of our meager front yard. This game, my survival skill, no one knew.

In this house of my dreams, we were the only occupants but, in the real one, another family lived upstairs. In order to get to our bathroom we had to go out into the hall where Mrs. Jones and her cotillion of drunken boyfriends staggered noisily up the stairs at all hours. The front door had no lock, and fear of this terrifying hallway made a bed wetter of me. Paralyzed on the spot, all the squeezing I could muster could not hold back the warm flow that flooded the feather mattress of the bed I often shared with Gran. Shame finally won out over fear. I would hold my breath, make sure I heard no sound coming from the front door, then sprint to the bathroom and upon arrival breathe a sigh of relief.

The Brady Street family had neither boundaries nor rules, not even lectures about peeing on Gran's mattress. Maybe they thought she did it. No one mentioned manners or proper behavior, or told me to do homework. Fortunately, my competitive nature pushed me to get high marks and shame gave me a voracious appetite to cultivate a middle-class look of "normalcy." I had to learn my own lessons about choices and consequences.

Weaving these early life memories together into a clear pattern has taken years. Like awakening in the morning to the awareness of a dream without being able to hang on to the fading image. Little fragments come but then slip away before the picture is fully formed. While writing, these recollections come much the same way. I wonder if I can trust these little shards that slip through the cracks. Tears flow easily at certain times, as old scenes come into view. Are those tears evidence of the mosaic's authenticity? I do not know the answer; I only know that I am driven to give words in service of fitting the pieces together in such a way as to uncover the truth—my truth.

My first therapist often said, "Chris, you will not get better until you stick your hands in the shit." It felt more like I was just backed into a stall, knee deep in muck with no safe way out. I kept digging, one small handful at a time. Eventually, little bits of insight would come, and then I'd gather the will to claw out a little more. And yet, now, scavenging in this dung heap feels like a holy calling. It seems as though my life began in the middle. Still, I have to go back to the beginning to make the patterns comprehensible to me, let alone anyone else.

******

At the convent, in the office of the Loretto Motherhouse, a wrestling match started in my head as soon as I took in the scene of this very Catholic, wholly-alien property. If the receptionist had given me the slightest indication that I was not welcome, I think I would have started sobbing and running back to my van. Thankfully, she acted as though I was expected and told me that Sister Elaine could not come to meet me at this time, but someone named "Susan" was on her way.

Will they see me as the phony that I know I am?
Surely they know that I am just masquerading as
a person on a spiritual quest. I know I look like a
pathetic fool. Do not let them see your insecurity;
just imitate them; act like you know what you are
doing, as though you do this all the time. These people
do not know me, for that matter, how could they? I
do not know me.

I gathered my luggage and followed Susan as she led me next door to one of the other red brick buildings. "This building used to be the dormitory for young women preparing to take vows in the religious life," Susan chattered. As we ascended the stairs, my anxiety level seemed to descend. The open space, wooden floors, and wide hall with its extra tall ceiling made me feel as though I had come up more than just one level. Everything about the building felt lofty—seemed appropriate. The spirits of sisters from bygone days surely lingered in the clean rooms filled with works of art, plants, and hand-sewn quilts. The place reeked of hospitality, as though it had all been arranged just for me.

Susan guided me into my room at the end of the hall, which was just across from a dorm style bathroom. Through two huge windows, I viewed the rural countryside—so different from my motel rooms of the past few days. "I'm in the best room in the building," I said appreciatively to Susan.

"Do you have any questions?" Did I ever! Susan had no idea how close she was to opening my existential Pandora's Box. Fifty-four years of unresolved philosophical issues clamored for answers. I restrained myself and opted for more basic questions: "Is there any specific schedule that I'll need to keep? What do I need to do?"

"You can do anything you wish," Susan replied. "The building next door, where the retired nuns live, is where you will find the dining room, the same one with the office where we just left. Meal times are posted, but you can fix food in the kitchen just down the hall. We require nothing. Welcome."

Is this paradise? It is quiet here and I do not have to do anything. I never want to ever leave!

All my normal distractions were back in Florida. There were no customers from my little specialty shops complaining or demanding my total attention in their search for the newest fashion. I had no employee pleading her case before me as to why she should not have to work every weekend. My mind did not race nor did my gaze scan the area to check for shifty-looking customers who might just drop a garment in their shopping bag and run off into the corridors of the mall. No, that life was finished. It did not follow me. Shoplifters, customers or employees now came and left as just a blur in my memory.

God, it is so quiet. Is this really me? Just four days ago, I left and set out on this whatever it is you call this trip—pilgrimage—insane quest. Who brought me to the backwoods of Kentucky and signed me up to hang out with nuns? I have no idea what I am doing here, but it sure feels better here than where I have been.

"Convent quiet" was different from the "not talking" kind of quiet that sometimes just happens. This silence was intentional. The contemplative energy penetrated to my very bones. I sensed a pulse in the building; it could be measured with a stethoscope. My first instinct was to just crawl into bed, pull one of those ancient quilts over my head and never go back to that other world.

Is this what I am supposed to do on retreat?

In the week to come, I did spend many hours curled up in that bed in a fetal position. I retreated. My body told me what to do: sleep. Intermittently, I would be guided by some force to take occasional treks to the kitchen for snacks. On one of those sandwich and tea missions, I intersected with Susan, my guide, and asked her, "How did you happen to arrive at Loretto?"

"I spent years down in Guatemala where I worked as a nurse," she said. "Now, I just hang out here and mostly spend my time writing."

She went on to share that she had grown up in a Quaker community. I knew a little about the Quaker practice of mostly silence in their gatherings.

I should have been born a Quaker. They know how to **do** *quiet; it's instinctual to them. I had to run away to find it. They just pay attention to it taking it with them wherever they go.*

I met another resident a few days later in the kitchen. We exchanged bits of our stories—me a runaway, she, a Baptist minister seeking renewal from her church in North Georgia.

"How did you come to be ordained in a church that is not exactly wide open to women ministers?" I queried.

Her answer stunned me. "I had an amazing mother," she said with pride. "And the greatest gift she gave me was a sense of my own personhood. She taught me that I could reach for any goal that I set for myself and do it without the need to have others' approval. I do not let the restrictions of my denomination stand in my way. I know who I am and what I am called to do."

Her statement went to my core. This word "personhood" clicked in my brain. It was not a concept normally batted around in my circles, let alone my family-of-origin.

Did I lack a sense of personhood? Why didn't Mama teach me that lesson? Could it be that I am on a search for that same kind of identity this woman secured so easily in her life. I want what she has—and I want it now!

Our little kitchen encounters became "burning bush" moments where I felt the urge to take off my shoes as if this were holy ground. The days I spent with the Sisters of Loretto put me in touch with a unique brand of holiness that I had never sensed was possible.

I had never heard of Thomas Merton, world-famous Trappist monk, writer, and mystic who, while living as a hermit in the nearby community of Gethsemane, wrote books on contemplation that were not yet on my shelf. Although the world of a now-deceased monk had opened its doors to me, I had far to go before I could even begin to navigate on my own. I needed guidelines and someone with experience to mentor me in understanding this new language. In my life, up until this point, contemplation had only been about pondering what styles would sell in my shops next season or figuring out how to get Mac to open up to me.

Silence, before, had been about thinking and making plans in the wee hours of the morning when sleep eluded me. The thought of *just being* had never entered the picture. Activity had defined me—I had energy enough for a dozen people. Mac often said, "Chris can get more done in a short time than anyone I have ever known." I loved my Super Woman image; it fed my ego. I knew the right words about humility and could repeat them as though they were sacred. When did that scorpion whip around and sting me? And, when did that immense fatigue take over and place me into this semi-comatose state?

Here, with these sisters, it surprised me to find I could actually adjust to a heretofore foreign pace, learn the steps to this new dance and then gracefully move to a new, slower beat. Although often alone, I never experienced loneliness. It felt at once natural, and yet equally unnatural to the way I had lived before. I had discovered a strong rhythm to life on the planet. I embraced this quiet and seemed to do it on purpose. I heard no nightly news and I had no checklist for the day—years of "dis-ease" were being neutralized and it required no effort from me. I accepted my solitude as a pure gift.

I took some meals in the dining room with the retired nuns along with a few other outsiders on retreat like me. The nuns looked somewhat like the women who lived in Mama's retirement building in Savannah, except for the few who still wore the traditional habits. I soon learned the drill: I could talk if I wished or I could choose a table for one and be quiet. Either choice was equally welcomed.

In the common dining room each day, I witnessed a very curious sight. An elderly nun would walk purposefully among the tables and into the kitchen with a two gallon bucket in her hand. She measured about five feet in height, just a little less in width, and wore the full, old-fashioned, black habit. Intent on her mysterious mission, she made no stops to visit with the other sisters. Her exit routine was as deliberate as her entrance, the bucket still in hand. My curious mind cooked up all the scenarios that might explain her strange ritual.

I hesitated to appear too nosy; after all, I am not a Catholic and was only a guest on their property. (Besides, I am a southerner and we hate to appear nosey, preferring to keep secret this universal compulsion.) Curiosity finally got the better of me. I gathered courage and questioned Elaine about the diminutive nun's puzzling routine. The answer turned out to be as simple as cat food: The mysterious bucket-toting creature lived as a hermit and, for whatever reason, cats seemed to find their way to her. The kitchen scraps fed her litter of thirty-plus strays.

This woman had a purpose and a calling. I had no idea what she did before she moved into the woods and sent out hospitality signals to homeless cats. After my stay, when I would question my own vocation, I'd think of that square little nun with her bucket and the singular devotion she gave to her daily task. Her image reminds me to bring my focus down to ground level and to quit looking so high. Feeding lots of cats each day could give a person all the satisfaction she needs. I suspect the cat sister did not feel an urgent need to get in a van and go searching for life's meaning as I was doing.

During my stay at Loretto, I learned that this order had founded schools in New Mexico and many of these women had been teachers of all sorts of ages and subjects. I noticed how grounded they were in the happenings of the moment. My own perception definitely picked up some kind of mystical healing energy. Nothing happened on a conscious level, of course, but I felt as though I merely sat in their classroom like an eager student, and soaked up lessons without words or lectures.

Silence did the teaching.

Two Women One Roof

*WHAT CAN WE GAIN BY SAILING TO THE MOON IF WE ARE
NOT ABLE TO CROSS THE ABYSS THAT SEPARATES US FROM
OURSELVES? THIS IS THE MOST IMPORTANT OF ALL
VOYAGES OF DISCOVERY, AND WITHOUT IT, ALL THE REST
ARE NOT ONLY USELESS BUT DISASTEROUS.*

THOMAS MERTON

Mama and Gran had no love for each other. "That woman is overbearing and hard to get along with," Mama frequently whispered to me, "I know she hates me." These conversations were always in hushed tones, in case Gran might be snooping close by, hoping to garner more evidence for her case against Mama.

By contrast, Gran did not speak softly when she wanted to give voice to her righteous grievances against Mama. "Mayme thinks her people are better than my people!" she would exclaim to anyone within earshot. Early on, I realized that both were absolutely right. Mama certainly came from a higher rung on the social ladder than the one she now precariously perched upon in the Young family. And no argument could be denied when it came to judging Gran as overbearing and difficult to get along with. Mama's unvoiced but definite opinion was quite evident: she knew, without a doubt, that the Boyds' bloodline was superior to the Youngs'.

Until I married and moved away, I acted as go-between for these two women, an integral noncombatant in their mostly silent, but raging war. I cannot recall even one tiny incident in which civil conversation passed between them. Each managed to give the other a wide berth in the close quarters they shared during food preparation.

Gran cooked pots of greens with fatback floating in the pot liquor (her word for the broth). She then made cornbread in a skillet, the same one that she baked teacakes in on other days. I have no idea how she made sugar, butter, vanilla and flour spooned into an iron skillet come out tasting so divine. I can still hear Gran slurping her bowl of pot liquor as she glared at Mama. Memory of the tasty teacakes helps sweeten the image.

High teatime on Brady Street with sweet iced tea.

Mama made chocolate pudding from a box mix for her dessert offering. Another of her specialties came in the form of a salad where she mixed canned tomatoes with saltines, then added sweet pickles and chopped hard-boiled eggs. She claimed the recipe came from some famous hotel. Mama believed the pink, soggy mound to be a unique delicacy, so much so that it became her offering at family reunions—some of the kin folks actually liked this Pepto Bismol look-alike concoction.

The cooking duels that waged daily at 117 Brady Street were high drama, but I can only catch the show in retrospect. At the time, I wanted to get as far away as possible from their second rate, tragi-comic performance. What surprises me today is the fact that I actually find cooking to be a therapeutic experience. Time in the kitchen is relaxed, never tense like that hot spot of my youth.

Mostly, I would name the relationship between these two women as "Great Mystery." I go fuzzy when trying to call back my feelings at the time when I was the main audience for them. I would like to think I loved this grandmother whose name I bear and whose genes gave me a large frame and height not found in Mama's people. When I allow myself to take an honest look in the mirror, I see Gran and some of her unlovable ways staring back.

Chris, there you are—ornery, overbearing and opinionated at times—damn, I hate that mirror. Old woman, go away!

I wish, now, that I had spent more time asking her to tell me the stories of her life. If I had known her better, I might not have been so quick to mimic her harsh ways— understanding might have saved me from being an unconscious devotee. And yet, her secrets would not have been so easy to uncover. A cold demeanor and isolating temperament made her unapproachable. Much of her day would be spent on the front porch, later reporting to whoever would listen about the number of cars she had counted during her time in the porch swing. This seemed to be her *raison d'etre*—a car census taker.

I am not that different from Gran when it comes to obsessive behavior. I don't count cars, but I do find that I go through meaningless motions of stacking, organizing and counting. If I feel stressed, my relief often comes when I go though every cabinet and closet and make sure each item is just where I think it belongs. Or, I play solitaire on the computer until all fifty-two cards turn over in the perfect sequence. All is, then, made right and I am a winner. Poverty and a hard life left Gran so scarred she could not let any warmth show through the vault she had created to protect herself, so it appears that her car counting routine must have given her a sense of control over the inhospitable environment of "home."

Gran did not like to be questioned. If I asked her about a piece of needlework in her hands, she would snap, "It's a *layoderler* to catch meddlers." I got the message: Don't meddle in Gran's business. To this day I can find no dictionary to define that word. When I wanted the front room for courting purposes, Gran took on the role of a *layoderler*. She would position herself in the center of the room, and stay until my date's ardor cooled and he gave up and left me with Gran snoring and firmly planted in her chair. As soon as my boyfriend left, off she would lumber in her felt slippers and chenille bathrobe. Guilt feelings can still crop up when I think of the many sinister plans I could dream up about how to remove her from the scene.

Why don't you go live with some other family, old woman?

My junior year in high school, 1952, television came into our home as it did to most of the neighbors. That "little box" with snowy pictures of strange people in it was to Gran, no doubt, paranormal. Her mesmerized body seldom left the front room. "Mayme's television has more preachers in it than Nell's does," she said, adding to the list of grievances she accumulated against another one of her daughters-in-law. For once, Mayme received praise—Gran's accolades for having the most preachers in a box.

Gran was born just two years after the Civil War ended. She certainly had every reason to distrust and be suspicious of her environment. There never came a doubt to her mind that Yankees added suffering to her rural poor family. Then came the Great Depression and, for sure, Herbert Hoover and

Republicans put them even deeper into poverty. Needless to say, Gran was a Democrat. When Eisenhower came on the screen with his Republican spiel, telling us why we should vote for him in 1952, Gran listened attentively to his every word. She did not see the war hero, the liberator, she only saw him as "the enemy," a "Republican," "damn Yankee." She stared straight into the TV and said, "Lying son of a bitch, he'll starve us all to death."

Each time I called up that scene from my memory bank, I'd smile and know that I still carry those same genes. Before I took my TV to Goodwill, I would scream at the "little box" when some "lying son of a bitch" tried to convince me that my safety and my freedom would remain intact if, again, we would invade and then occupy another piece of foreign soil. This shared political point of view continues to be the closest I've come to feeling any warmth for the large woman who hovered around in my world and interfered in my personal business.

It is difficult for me to put myself into these ancient scenes of my life. I viewed my part to be that of a peeping Tom character who peered in a window, definitely a bit-player in the family drama. I have no idea if that is the way childhood feels to others; I only know I played the role of an invisible witness, an outsider doing her best to see through the cloudy pane.

"Love" was not a word in the vocabulary of our household other than in reference to something one was craving, something like some ice cream. "Wouldn't you love to have a cone of cream?" Mama might say. "Run down to the store and get us one." I do not recall ever hearing the love word connected with a person, definitely not me—ice cream, yes, never *the young'uns* in the house. If ever I felt love for Gran, or for any folks who lived within those same walls, I lacked the way to discover or even name the feeling.

I have tried to see a clear pattern from this period of my life, but the parts keep fragmenting and shifting, like shards of murky glass in a kaleidoscope. I would like to have this whole "question of love" and "relationship with family" feel less ambiguous. I claim to love mystery but, the truth is, I want these pieces to fit together. I want to be able to focus, see more clearly. I want to know the truth beyond these ephemeral fragments.

My struggle to define "family love" has always puzzled Mac. "Masochistic," he called it. "Why do you put yourself through such contortions and do all this crazy self-examination?" He often heard me sob, "I am not sure that I have ever loved anyone." To Mac, this sounded so harsh. To me, "love" was much too complex to ever know it without a doubt. The concept must be dusted off and redefined at least quarterly if not daily. Mac just stared at me when these emotional tantrums took over; he had no reference book to help him understand my condition.

I bought a painting at an art show entitled *Freeing up the Self.* The Picasso-like figures look contorted and misshapen. It took me only one minute to shell out the dollars to pay for this piece; I had to have it. I continue to find myself staring at it as it reminds me of the twisted positions I have taken on this, as yet, unfinished journey to liberation: my quest to learn how to love.

I am convinced that we come into life with a certain mission and our own unique road map. Mine has caused me to turn upside down, sideways and twist every which way in order to see exactly what fork in the road I should take next.

******

At the convent, I met for spiritual direction each day with Sister Elaine, a woman near my own age. Nothing about her fit the preconceived notion I had previously held about women who chose to live the celibate life. She gave off an earthy appearance in her jeans and sneakers, never the image of an uptight nun who might rap your knuckles if you gave the wrong answer.

I needed this woman to point me in a new direction, but the concept of "spiritual direction" was uncharted territory. My Methodist Church never made mention of this service to parishioners. We had preachers, choir directors, organists and even a Christian Education person, but no Spiritual Director. At weddings, a director stood at the back of the church and told the groomsmen and bridesmaids when to walk down the aisle; the word "spiritual"—let alone curious or supportive— did not show up in this job description.

I enrolled in a new school when I came to Loretto. Elaine and I met in her book-lined office each afternoon. I had only to walk down two flights of stairs from my third floor room. I arrived with some measure of apprehension; my perpetual need for a script was left wanting. I had no idea what to say and could not find words to tell her why I had landed on her doorstep. The easy thing would have been to talk about the books surrounding us; they were her trademark.

I bumbled my way through and found enough coherent words to let Elaine in on the happenings in the inner recesses of my mind, at least the ramblings I had access to. Miraculously, she helped me unscramble and put order to them. I actually seemed to be saying something that she appeared to think made perfect sense. She even quoted scripture to match my mixed-up thoughts, suggesting that I spend time reading and meditating on the instructions Jesus gave to his disciples when he sent them to cast out unclean spirits and to heal disease.

THESE TWELVE JESUS SENT OUT,
CHARGING THEM...
RAISE THE DEAD, CLEANSE LEPERS, CAST OUT DEMONS...
TAKE NO GOLD, NOR SILVER,
NOR COPPER IN YOUR BELTS...
NOR TWO TUNICS, NOR SANDALS...
AND IF ANYONE WILL NOT RECEIVE YOU...
SHAKE OFF THE DUST FROM YOUR FEET AS YOU LEAVE.

MATTHEW 10:5-14

What does she want me to learn from this scripture? I am the one who needs healing. I sure as hell did not set out on this trek to lay my hands on anyone—me a healer? She must be crazy. I don't get it. I need to be raised from the dead. Excuse me!

Benevolence had not been my motivation for striking out, the only sick person I could think of healing was me, not even Mac. I had failed at my feeble attempt to resurrect anyone, let alone the dead. Then that part about no silver or gold sure did not apply, I had my gold credit card. As for no extra clothing, I had to have my boots and just a few extra changes of jeans and sweat shirts. But the part about shaking the dust from your sandals when you did not feel welcomed, *that* struck a chord I could hear.

Did I shake off the dust of Quincy, Florida? Could I condense my urge to get out of town down to something so simple and basic? I had managed with my outsider status for years, so what had changed? Why now?

When we first moved to Quincy in 1970, I felt as though I had come to my soul home. Mac's parents loved me and took me in as a daughter. They would have been the parents of my choice; I became the child of my dreams. We lived with them in the bungalow in which they had raised their four boys. His mother had confessed that she truly lived for the day her third son would return to the family fold. Little did we know she meant it, literally. Her death came just a few months after we moved in with them. Waiting for our arrival kept her cancer at bay until we were there to help Papa adjust to the loss of the love of his life.

"Shaking the dust" of those days is not something I've ever wished to do. Quincy had been the right place to live at that time. Greg, our only child, twelve years old, flourished in this "hometown" environment with lots of cousins. The warmth of this large family satisfied yearnings I did not even know I'd had. I remember telling Mac, with tears in my eyes, "I have never felt so much like I am right where I belong." I focused my attention on my business venture, the retail ladies' clothing store. But the truth of 1970 did not match the truth of 1991. Needs change, just like the seasons. I had, for sure, stepped into a new season of my life.

Although the answers did not come at Loretto Motherhouse, the haranguing voice in my head went totally silent for the first time—ever. In the Kentucky countryside, I found my little *niche*, accidental as it seemed. This spot must have been prepared just for me, and on the day I made the call to Elaine (by now I had her permission to drop the "Sister" word) my action set the rest in motion. I could retreat, relax and allow life to unfold as it wished.

The serenity sent energy pulsing through my *being*. Sensual is the only word that comes to mind. I saw, heard, tasted and smelled life in ways that my body had never before experienced.

I found peace that certainly passed my limited understanding.

Then There's Sam

*FORGIVENESS DOES NOT CHANGE THE PAST, BUT IT DOES
ENLARGE THE FUTURE*

PAUL BOESE

THE FLAWS I SAW IN Daddy could probably be linked to the fact that Mildred Christine birthed him. I judged him as insecure, weak, and vain; certainly an under-achiever. Most likely, Gran emasculated him early on with her dark, controlling ways.

Daddy built himself up by applying labels to others; he used all the ethnically derogatory terms to describe people that didn't look like him. I thought "damn Irish" was one word until I was grown and out of Savannah, a place over-flowing with "damn Irish." Daddy's folks came from the backwoods of Georgia and South Carolina. We had no traceable family tree, as far as I could tell. Like a scrawny bald cypress, the Young family just sprang up out of the Okefenokee Swamp.

"He's a big shot," Daddy would spout in one of his frequent rants. He said the words with a tone of disgust, but, at the same time, appeared to be proud of the fact that he actually knew this man. A woman never held this exalted position—"uppity" would be the word he used to describe a female big shot. His membership in the Masons, that group of men who passed on ancient secrets and wore funny hats, caused him to brush up against quite a few of these "big shots." I never knew exactly where the line fell between those folks and the ordinary, everyday people. I suspect a big shot was any man who wore a coat and tie to work.

Daddy and both of my brothers worked for National Gypsum, a place where rocks from Nova Scotia came in on huge ships so they could be crushed and then turned into wallboard, also known as sheet rock. Early in my life, I knew all the terminology about the process. Conversations in our household, when the three men were at home, consisted of animated talk about machines breaking down on the night shift or numbers of feet of sheet rock shipped that day from the warehouse where daddy was in charge. Sammy took advantage of the "GI Bill" and enrolled in engineering school at Georgia Tech. He came home summers to work. Hap stayed on the job that he had started at the age of sixteen.

My brothers were my heroes. I did not know anyone at 38th Street School who had a brother in college. I loved to throw out that little bit of information any time I could. Hap, the high school dropout, had style and charisma that kept a string of women hanging around hoping for a glance of him. For a period of time, Hap was the only one in the family with a car. This fact definitely added to his popularity in our transportation-poor community.

My family moved up the social ladder when Sammy completed his degree at Tech and became the plant engineer. He then quickly rose to the top as the plant manager. "The Youngs" had arrived!

Daddy's most attractive and predictable quality was his gift for seeing the best in his children. He would bore people with his endless bragging about our accomplishments, none of which were particularly noteworthy except, of course, for Sammy's rise to the top with National Gypsum. That promotion put Daddy in "Big Shot" heaven.

Daddy bequeathed his swearing gene to me. His colorful words continue to roll so easily from my mouth—they are always delicious. My Southern Baptist sister at one time expressed concern that I had also picked up the alcohol addiction. She suspected my daily glass or two of red wine represented only the tip of my problem. Actually, none of us seemed to stumble into that dependence.

No matter how hard I search the old records of my family, I can't find many images of Daddy that are filed under the "happy memory" heading. Other family members, I see with some degree of humor—Daddy? Nada. I wish I could do a little hocus-pocus and make his senseless antics materialize as comedy. For now, I am stuck with an image that still has sharp edges.

Stay back, Chris. This could hurt. Remember that icky feeling that always came over you when Daddy walked in the room. Why that visceral response? Your body seems to know something that the brain cannot name.

I did not find it funny, for example, when I was left alone in the car with images of monsters banging on the windows, while Daddy and his bowling buddies were in a bar getting soused. No one in the family heard the story of my night of terror in that black car. Mama did not ask, "Where have you been since the bowling league finished?"

Mayme remained, as always, true to her "ask no questions" commitment.

What are mamas good for if not to ask questions and then do the mama thing and scare those monsters away? I have no idea what I would have told her if she had asked. It might have made her cry. I don't want her to see me cry and I damn sure do not want her to be sad, anymore than she already is.

Sometimes Daddy would take me to a Vaudeville stage show in downtown Savannah where we'd sit for hours watching bawdy and vulgar performers. He thought they were hilarious, I didn't. Sitting there felt as agonizing as being in a car while mean creatures were clawing at the windows. On the positive side, those shows were in the Lucas movie theater, and when the live performance finished, the curtain opened to the movie screen. That's when the magic started, the moment I had waited for—glamorous people, costumes, dancing and music, Betty Grable or Donald O'Connor tap dancing across the screen.

Daddy probably had a flask in his pocket on those occasions, so he stayed sufficiently drunk and completely clueless about the damage done by taking an underage child to tasteless live performances. However the interior of the theater was not shabby, far from it. I loved the ornate Victorian lavishness of Savannah's old movie houses, and would suffer through whatever it took to have my elegant night at the picture show. The red carpet, the brass rail up the wide staircase, the elaborate Baroque molding along with the overhanging box seats, kept me enthralled as we were escorted by a uniformed usher carrying a small flashlight. The distance back to Brady Street measured just over a mile, but, to me, it felt as though I had been lifted off the planet.

My other outings with Daddy were to Grayson Stadium to watch the Savannah Indian baseball games. We had our spot behind first base, up in the bleachers. Daddy appeared to be sober on those nights. He took on the role of a serious teacher when he explained the ins and outs of the game. Back on Brady Street, he often got out the bat and ball and put on his coaching hat. In the alley behind the house, pitching to me, Sam took on a different persona. "You're swinging like a girl," was the only admonishment I needed to make me correct my stance and follow through like a home-run slugger. Thanks to these practice sessions I became the best hitter on the block. When giving baseball tips on batting, throwing a ball or explaining the rules, Sam became a confident and capable man. I longed to have that daddy all the time.

But eventually, as day turned to night, Sam would revert to slurring words, loud cussing, and behaving like a silly drunk relative that I did my best to hide from my friends. I never saw him stagger or fall down on the sidewalk or do any of the obvious moves that would make his condition apparent. He merely talked non-stop and not one word made sense. He launched into tirades about some SOB at work who had done something that pissed him off; Mama could only make one of her ineffectual statements with a grimace, "Now Sam." If he even heard her benign admonishment, it did not stop the rant.

I hated listening to his endless rages, but found his swear words flowing easily from my own mouth by the time I was eight years old. I needed no help from a hidden bottle to trigger my verbal rage.

Why is it that what I dislike most in another is the same thing I find myself doing? I question whether this ability of mine to see this kind of connection is a gift or a curse. The knowledge of the source does not cause me to clean up my act.

Daddy, a handsome man, wore a hat and double-breasted suit when he had an occasion to dress up. On the rare occasions that our family found its way to church, he looked like a big shot. He had an amazing gift for math, and his handwriting and speech could make one think he had some measure of higher education. In fact, he went only as far as the sixth or seventh grade in school. Coming from the backwoods of Georgia was undetectable in terms of stereotypical country folk's speech. Occasionally some grammatical error slipped out, like "I seen."

If I needed help with math, Daddy would have been my man. However, I never did. Math came to me as if by osmosis—I loved it. I now know that was the best gene that came from the Young's, well maybe my height, too. Daddy's brothers were both tall and worked in businesses where their math skills were used. Daddy could walk through the warehouse at National Gypsum and figure in his head exactly how many square feet of wallboard was there ready to be shipped out. This image of my tall, thin handsome daddy, calculating in his head could get filed in that empty "good memory" folder.

The last days of Daddy's life reminded me of something a psychologist friend once said. I asked Julian about changes that happen when a person has dementia or a stroke and how he thought they appeared "to become someone else." He said, "I believe the person just becomes more of whatever they already were."

Daddy lapsed into dementia in the last two years of his life. His goofy rhetoric seemed to be all that was left, gone was the walking calculator and the handsome swagger that could have been Sam. In its place we had a skinny, blank-look-on-his-face man that no one could manage, certainly not Mayme. Mama handled his malady with her usual penchant for fantasy: she thought every hallucination and bit of nonsense that he'd utter contained some deep meaning embedded in code. She spent her days concocting all sorts of stories around his limitations. Mama did not drive, so accepting Sam's inability to navigate the highways was not easy. She could not bring herself to say, "Sam, you cannot drive and we need to get rid of this car." Instead she told him, "The car needs a part and the garage has it on order. It will be here soon." The story helped her to hang on to the possibility that Daddy would come to his senses and snap out of this new brand of craziness.

When Daddy died in 1981, I was forty-four years old, and if he had been able to remember who I was in those last months, he would still have introduced me as his baby. The baby label is humiliating when you are twelve years old. In my forties the tag was ludicrous, especially since my siblings took after Mama's kin with that short of stature build or "squatty" as Mama would say of herself. My body could be described as "chunky," something that made me feel like a baby elephant around my squatty family.

Daddy died the day before Saint Patrick's Day, a major event in Savannah. His body was in the funeral home just across from Forsythe Park, the final stop of the parade. At this point in the huge celebration, green beer flowed like water. The "damnirish" had the whole family trapped across town. We could not get there to greet folks who also could not get there to stand vigil with the body. The viewing had to be delayed until streets barricades were removed and all the drunks staggered home.

When we finally made our way to the grand old house on Drayton Street—the home of Fox and Weeks Funeral

Home—Frances, Sammy and Hap gathered round the coffin and cried together. I stayed in the background and felt guilty. I could not and would not join them. Instead, I enjoyed the grandeur of the setting and remembered all the times I had played in the "big park." My friends on Brady Street never said, "Let's go to Forsythe Park," it was always the "big park" to us.

I do not stand over dead bodies and gaze at the lifeless shell of a person. They are not there. Why would I want to focus on closed eyes that cannot see me? In the same way, I do not visit cemeteries. I see no reason to hang around with the buried remains of the departed. I'll just play my own little fantasy game here and, by the way, Sam, I'm not a baby.

The next day, I walked into the church for the funeral and saw all the flowers laced with leftover green carnations, I had to control my giggle response. The image of Sam cussing the "damnirish" took over my being.

Gotcha, old man! You wouldn't see the humor—I do.

The Masons, Daddy's secret brotherhood, circled around the grave at Bonaventure Cemetery, each with a little apron tied around his paunchy middle. They spoke words, possibly profound, that I could not decode. I assumed Mama understood this gibberish. Maybe The Eastern Star, the women Masons, knew some of the secrets and spoke this same language. I stood in a catatonic state staring off at the swampy surroundings that were not far from our old housing project home, the one we moved into after Brady Street.

Sam's sendoff perfectly matched the story of his life with Mayme. The grave scene put the finishing touch on their relationship, a union made in the fantasy world of their odd imaginations. He and Mama taught me well, though I choose different fantasies from theirs. Life is a stage, I just tap dance to a different beat. I dealt with my Daddy's death by finding a therapist, something no one in the family had ever conceived a possibility.

The baby makes strange choices.

******

At the end of my allotted week in the convent, I put "New Kentucky Home," in my rear view mirror and pointed the van towards Albuquerque, another step into the unknown. My plans for this next stop were vague. I'd been promised a bed for five nights at The Center for Action and Contemplation. They had some interns who were there for long periods, but they also had a bit of space for strays. Once again, I had no idea what to expect. My connection had been with their founder, Richard Rohr, a Franciscan priest. I'd been listening to his lectures on tapes for months. I had to meet this man. Rohr had given language to many of the undecipherable messages that played in my internal receiver. He had introduced me to a version of Jesus completely different from the one I'd first encountered in Sunday school. This Jesus did not require me to bow down before him; rather, he spoke a message of peace, of a new order.

Rohr moved Jesus out of the cute little story book, white-washed images from my childhood, to a man who had real substance—real flesh and blood, not that filmy, ghost-of-a-guy. This message left out the sentimental, baby Jesus born in a manger, and instead connected with the metaphors from the story: the lowly birth, the desert temptations, the stand against powers of domination and control and, most important, the mystery of incarnation—embodiment. Rohr awakened in me my ability to sit with mystery, and yet he gave clarity around the story and history of the "fully human" Jesus.

Thinking about this next stop energized me, even though details about the place and people I would encounter remained vague. I felt excitement and anticipation, unlike the anxiety I had felt before my arrival at the convent. This time I felt no fear; I knew I could relax and accept whatever came with the unfamiliar surroundings. My ignorance had turned to bliss.

I traveled back roads with few signs and less evidence of what might lay ahead. The interstates did not work on my unconventional journey. *I Believe in What I Feel* became my traveling song. That day in Memphis, when I first heard it played on the radio, the DJ introduced it as the number one bluegrass song of the week. I tried to find it in music stores all over Memphis and no one had ever heard of it, nor could they find it in any catalog. Is it possible the radio was not on in the car, that instead the song was being beamed down from lord knows where?

New Mexico, "Land of Enchantment," land of enlightenment, and land of people who march to the music of a different drummer. One of my favorite icons of this place, Georgia O'Keefe, once said, "If you come to New Mexico, it will itch you for the rest of your life." Carl Jung's experience of "oneness with all things" came to him when he visited Taos. Those two testimonials put me in good company.

I arrived at Tepayac, the house owned by The Center for Action and Contemplation. As I walked onto the porch, two women who were lounging and reading there, assured me that I had, in fact, come to the right place. One of them looked longingly at my van and asked, "Could we go out and eat pizza? This place is totally vegetarian, and I would kill for some pepperoni or Italian sausage."

As we shared pizza and got to know each other, I found another "new family." These two women were "runaways" also. One was a social worker, the other a graduate student in Pastoral Counseling at Loyola in New Orleans. They, too, were searching for signs of life and a community to help them uncover their next steps. Like me, they had been listening to Rohr's teaching tapes.

For half-an-hour each morning, I'd meditate with my group of housemates and then do some of the housekeeping chores. The "real" interns treated me as though I belonged. I cooked, cleaned, gardened and stood with them in silent peace demonstrations. As the name of the Center implied, there was an equal focus on social action and contemplation in this community.

I've found my real family. Can't believe it, they do not seem to find me the least bit strange. Have I moved into someone else's body? If I never went back, would anyone come looking for me?

The Other Side

THE UNIVERSE IS FULL OF MAGICAL THINGS PATIENTLY WAITING FOR OUR WITS TO GROW SHARPER.

EDEN PHILPOTTS

L IFE ON BRADY STREET HAD its upsides from ages three to thirteen: going barefoot, playing ball in the street or on the vacant lot behind the house, riding my bike all over Savannah without having anyone come looking for me. The outside world matched my inner world where the word adventure was *writ large*.

The sidewalks were made for roller-skating. A string around my neck kept the skate key secure until needed to tighten the piece that attached the skates to my shoes. To perform any "fancy stuff," I had to turn the key to the point that the sole of the shoe sometimes separated from the upper—a small price to pay for the thrill of such extraordinary feats as being able to zip down the sidewalk, turn backwards at just the right moment in front of Calvary Baptist Social Hall, and sail off the curb into Barnard Street.

My brother, Hap, perfected this stunt, an amazing spectacle; I delighted in gathering the neighborhood gang to watch my big brother. I had learned my first lesson in goal setting as I witnessed his graceful landing. I visualized the time when I would replicate his agile moves. I had seen the starlet and award-winning figure skater Sonja Henie perform her poised leaps and twirls in movies. She didn't have to worry about a collision with the Barnard Street bus—a major concern for Hap.

The day my skating dream became a reality, I thought I might as well die on the spot; life would never be better. There are times when I think that may have been the peak experience of my life. I can still feel the freedom of becoming airborne, and most gloriously staying upright with grace, just like Sonja.

That Barnard Street bus presented a hazard when sailing off the Brady Street curb. Other times it served as the getaway car. When I could come up with a quarter, the bus transported me to the picture shows. Five cents went for the ride and fifteen cents bought the movie ticket. If I walked one way, the other nickel could buy popcorn. This is still the formula I use for all my financial dealings. I often ponder, "Do I want to walk or will I buy popcorn?"

Mama took charge of Daddy's paycheck. In spite of her poor money-management skills, she kept the family treasury. Daddy had his drinking money and Mama managed the rest. I call this arrangement the inept leading the drunk. However, she gets the credit for our Brady Street escape. Mayme convinced the city Housing Authority that we qualified for subsidized housing—a four-bedroom duplex in the projects.

We had been on Brady Street for ten years. I was thirteen when we moved to Savannah Gardens. I actually had a room of my own, my very own double bed and no bed mate. My own closet, too! There were none in the old house and here we each had one where the contents were concealed by a curtain. We had a fuel oil heater in the hall, and a washing machine in the kitchen so the clothes did not have to be scrubbed and then wrung out; they were almost dry when you hung them on the line in the back yard.

I rode the city bus from the housing project back to Richard Arnold Junior High. Mama's skills for rosily reframing reality came in handy. She said she would not let the school know we had moved, so I would not have to transfer to a different Junior High. I could also ride my bike from Savannah Gardens (not as lush and landscaped as the name might imply) back to the old neighborhood. The move brought added freedom. My world expanded.

It did not take long to make friends in my new neighborhood, many of them a year or two older. The boys in the group called themselves "The Dirty Dozen." Several were good athletes and, of course, being able to bounce or throw a ball often means you are someone special. I loved those guys; they were, indeed, special. We hung out together and went to the dances on Friday night at the community center. The black radio station played our music of choice. We spoke in coded messages, using words from the DJs or quoting sexual innuendos from lyrics. This gang brought me up-to-date on the ways of the world—nothing was off limits. We knew who was "doing it" and who was not, without judgment—ordinary life in the housing project.

Savannah had only two public high schools in the 1950s—for the white kids, that is. Savannah High had the usual curriculum and Commercial High, where many of my friends were going, taught skills like typing and shorthand. I chose Savannah High, not because I expected to go to college, but because the thought of becoming a secretary had no appeal. I had been a top student in my first seven years in school, but by the eighth year I made a conscious choice to give up being smart. Like so many girls in their early teens, especially at this time, I thought smart was not cool, so I chose image over intelligence.

My first day at Savannah High opened a door to another world—fourteen years old and starting the 10th grade—and the school, only about two miles from Brady Street and just a little farther from the project, might as well have been Jupiter. Most of the students there were alien to me. They came from the "right" side of the tracks and lived in those big houses where the maids had to enter by the back door. I had heard of such people, but now they became names and faces in my classroom.

I do not remember aspiring to live in that "other side of the tracks" world, but damn, I wanted to dress like *them*. I would have sold my soul for a pair those black, soft ballet-type shoes with the narrow strap around the ankle. Oh how I wanted to cruise the halls of Savannah High in a pair of those magic slippers. Watching and noticing their ways made an indelible imprint, becoming my primary education at Savannah High.

At the height of my assent to "cool," Jay Helmken shagged (the dance of the time) into my life. He still holds the record for the coolest white guy I have ever known. We lived in a segregated world, so cool and black was not in the running then. Jay was all fire with red hair to match his flaming personality; an aura of poetry and art surrounded him. My heart still races when I think of those sultry nights when his freckled hot hands put me in touch with my own body. I adored him, and for the first time in my life, I felt visible, **yes,** desired. That visibility had heat and a palpable pulse that I'd craved. He found spaces in my body I did not even know existed. I suspect most fifteen-year-olds lack the sensual knowledge we displayed in that very steamy year. I only know that he unleashed an unholy yearning in me for more of the same. I was starved for anyone to pay attention to me, to see me, to touch me, to enliven and awaken my senses. And touch me he did—it was electric. Jay Helmken brought out in me the qualities that I'll always think of as my best.

Our romance began on the day he parked his bike in front of the house, came to my door and yelled for me to come out, "Hey Chris, hop on my bike and let's go to the soda shop and play *Sixty Minute Man* on the jukebox," he said. The year was 1952 and the lyrics of the song were shocking.

A sixty-minute man, they call me loving Dan, I rock'em roll'em all night long, I'm a sixty-minute man. They call me lovin' Dan.

Then come explicit descriptions of each fifteen-minute interval in the hour, the last being, *"fifteen minutes of blowing my top"*. Even for those of us who could not as yet comprehend the message, we knew we were being pulled in the direction of that beat. The memory still causes my heart to flutter and my temperature to rise. Jay gave me a wild ride and a new image. He swept me up and carried me off on the back of his bike, I became Eve—eating up that apple. Life took on whole new hues in an already complex pattern.

Jay was my vehicle out of the dreary bleakness of the housing project and into the world of art and passion for life. For many years our paths did not cross, and then, by chance, we had a brief connection when we were both in our early 50's. We met for lunch in New Orleans, where he was designing floats for Mardi Gras. The years had not doused his fire. He walked up to our meeting place with the old familiar bounce in his step. The red hair was concealed by a planter's straw hat. He wore an island shirt and looked like the boat captain just back from the Caribbean, where he had, in fact, spent most of his adult life. The talk over lunch led us to speculate about what might have been. He said, "If you had married me, I know how it would have been—you would have a divorce on your record and I would have five instead of four."

"Jay, I knew that when I was fifteen." I stared into his blue-green eyes and caught the look of surprise there. "The thought of spending the rest of my life with you did not cross my mind. I could not name it at that point, but I knew that flame of yours could never be contained by one woman; you do not have the faithful gene. I wanted more than the 'sixty-minute' experience you offered." We both laughed. I had no regrets. I cannot remember what we ate; I only know my whole body feasted on the sweetness of the memories wafting from that table. We parted outside the restaurant and I never laid my eyes on him again. The spark he ignited still glows.

Jay is my clearest memory of those high-school years; much of the rest is rather fuzzy, sort of dreamlike. There were sororities for which I'd known I would never qualify. I could not imagine presenting myself into any world I had to be voted into. I was an outsider and "getting in" was never my goal. I was shooting "higher": make some money, buy a great looking outfit, and get out of Savannah—real big stuff. The steps to attaining these goals were not clear to me then.

When I tell people that I grew up in Savannah, they swoon. Everyone thinks it is such a wonderful place. And they are right—I just know a different Savannah. When I left in 1957, the waterfront, now a tourist destination, was a place of foreign sailors, bars, and brothels. The high-society, sorority girls played the game of hanging out in the waterfront bars; they loved the low-life novelty of drinking and smoking in a slummy setting. The intrigue of crummy places and juke joints eluded me. I guess I would have to be in a sorority to understand the foreign charm.

This disparity between the slums and Savannah's upper crust gave insight that now forms my worldview. Those were formative years for me and I am grateful for my gift of navigating my way between two opposite poles of Southern American culture. From this experience, I have a sense that there is an unseen parallel world right here, the same way the "other world" in Savannah was there all the while that I lived on Brady Street and in the projects. It might as well have been an unseen world, because I never saw it until I stepped into the halls of Savannah High.

******

As I left Tepayac and set out for California, the same feeling I had experienced on the day I left Kentucky washed over me.

> *I could stay here forever. This new pattern of quiet autonomy is addictive. Damn it! Why are the good feelings about the day always tainted by thoughts that soon I must return to that old life. Can I fit back in that brace? Shut up! Can't you just be quiet and let me enjoy a moment of peace?*

The van had everything I needed—music, NPR news, food and a gadget to heat water for my coffee. I could make a cup without even changing my speed. I felt powerful. All my basic needs were met.

Still, thoughts of Mac and my other home lingered on the edge of my awareness. The daily calls gave almost no information; I just felt his draining sadness coming through the line. I only knew I needed to become stronger, fortified in my "practice," serene and secure about *me* before I could extend energy outside myself to help Mac. Words to express this thought did not flow from me, but in the place where language did not exist, I understood. I lived beyond language; my inner-navigation skills kept pointing the way. This pilgrimage made no sense when I tried to speak about it, my gut knew, not my head.

Out of this filmy fog where thoughts of Mac resided in my consciousness came the memory of a dream from the recent past:

I was on a kiddy train, the kind that people ride in at amusement parks or zoos. I jumped in the front seat, oblivious to the fact that I had chosen the position of the driver. I quickly learned that the locomotion of this vehicle depended on me. My feet had to go in a laundry type sack with the string tied around my knees. My job was to keep my feet moving so that power would be generated to move the wheels. The action of my feet and calves was frantic, like a toddler having an out-of-control tantrum. To further complicate my responsibilities there were passengers in the rear and I had to navigate on city streets and get us safely through busy intersections. I managed to stay focused in my hobbled, agitated condition, while knowing, without a doubt, that this task was way more than I bargained for when I jumped on the train. I maintained a hyper-vigilant condition to keep up the pressure in the sack while staying alert to traffic along the route. Eventually, we all arrived safely at our destination which turned out to be Savannah Beach, Tybee Island. Once there, I was joined by old friends for a house party. They had a surprise for me—J.D. Salinger, my favorite author, was to join us.

The reliving of that dream boosted my spirits with its "all shall be well" message. And yet, in my power steering, automatic transmission vehicle, I felt as though I had my feet in a sack and folks were sitting behind me expecting me to transport us all to a safe spot. I just kept peddling and muddling my way through with my compass pointing west instead of east as my prophetic dream imaged—made me wonder about the possibility that I had misread the signs.

Should I be sitting on the Atlantic Ocean instead of heading to the Pacific? Who will surprise me at the end of the line? Will I miss my chance to hang out with my fellow escape artist, J. D. Salinger?

War, Workin' & Wishin'

*IF YOU WANT TO BUILD A SHIP, DON'T HERD PEOPLE
TOGETHER TO COLLECT WOOD AND DON'T ASSIGN THEM
TASKS AND WORK BUT RATHER, TEACH THEM TO LONG
FOR THE ENDLESS IMMENSITY OF THE SEA.*

ANTOINE DE SAINT-EXUPÉRY

THE KOREAN WAR KIND OF crept up on my family. It had started in 1950 and before we knew it, my easy going, fun loving, darling brother Hap had to leave us and go fight for god knows what in that odd place. President Truman called it a "police action." Police action or war, call it what you will, Hap got drafted. He, like Sammy, did what the young men of the time did—they served. Who or what they served, I had no idea.

*Who are those people? Where is Korea? I have never
even heard of such a country. Why are we there?
What have they done to us?*

There were no blackouts during those war years, but I sure as hell stayed in the dark about the reasons for our involvement. The pain and craziness of my country registered. My gut knew that Hap did not belong there in such senseless killing.

Why were we fighting and what could we possibly gain? War does not make sense.

I knew young men were dying there and, to the best of my knowledge, nothing was being gained for anybody. I know that today, North Korea continues to be a loose-cannon, and if anything significant came from the bloodshed of that "police action" I do not know what it was.

Every year of my life has been filled with some war or threat of war, and I cannot fit this fact into my consciousness, there is always an asterisk there that sends me to a footnote that only adds to the confusion. If decade after decade of war makes sense, then I really am the insane one. If not, then we deserve to be protected from the insanity of those who wield this costly and bloody power.

Hap returned and again was the generous brother who shared his car and the loose change on his dresser. He went back to the plant on the river, where he worked swing shifts. There were times when Hap would go missing for days at a time and I would hear Daddy telling Mama that he had been at work, but other than that bit of news, his whereabouts were unknown. His alibis always began with the words, "This 'old boy' and I..." But the calls he got at home were never from some "old boy"—they were definitely female. I loved his freewheeling ways and longed for his courage. He and I had the reputation in the family for being the "wild ones." I remember overhearing Mama telling one of her friends, "I did okay raising my first two children, but these last two are killing me." We obviously were in no hurry to finish her off, since she lived over forty years beyond that day.

General Eisenhower became President during my junior year in high school. The great soldier made us feel secure. Whoopee! Let the good times roll. The "happy family"

TV shows began to mirror back to us who we thought we were supposed to be, what we aspired to. My family's basic needs were met, but we did not flourish. No one spoke of future plans at all, let alone encouraged me to think of adulthood other than a vague insinuation about "the right man." Certainly, my only focus was the boyfriend of the moment, my next date, or what I would wear.

When I graduated at the age of seventeen, I went to work in the Liberty National Bank where evidence of my weekly salary could be found in my closet. My need for order was satisfied when both sides of the ledger balanced at the end of each workday, and I did not hate sitting in my little cage handling large sums of cash. Plus, I could do this job on the corner of Bull and Broughton Streets, the epicenter of Savannah.

My last year with the bank took me to the Hunter Air Force Base branch, where I had my first, true glimpse of the military world. Those jobs on the base usually went to married women, but my guardian angel knew where I needed to be.

In spite of loving my job, I also quickly learned there was no hope for a better position in the bank—the highest-ranking female was the head bookkeeper; there were no women officers. My starting salary in 1954 was thirty-five dollars a week—a little more than eighty-five cents per hour. By the end of three years, it had risen to fifty dollars a week. The meager earnings gave me no options except to live at home with my parents and Gran and, without this arrangement, my wardrobe certainly would have suffered.

My tether was short, but I sure looked good.

Frances had worked in this same bank in the forties and tells my favorite story about the night all the bookkeepers were working late to get statements out. The building had no air conditioning in those days, and the women were all alone in their second-floor workspace. They came up with a daring, scandalous plan to cool their bodies: they took off their dresses and finished the task wearing only their slips.

I love to muse on that image; it would make a great movie scene. Right there in that tall phallic-symbol-of-a-building, the whole bookkeeping department worked furiously on the oversized noisy machines, sweating though their filmy underwear, over too-tight girdles meant to cover over the "flaws" that movie starlets were spared. Still, nothing could stop them from hustling to keep a job that was as high as they would ever go in this man's world of finance. This picture tells volumes about those days and the world of women—working women, that is.

My last boss at the bank was a Vice President whom I thought had the IQ of a turnip. He loved to strut around and let his importance show. I saw him as a cartoon character and could amuse myself by imagining him being forced to work overtime to get his books balanced, while stripped down to his skivvies.

When my bank day ended, I entertained myself by going to the city league softball games where Daddy and both my brothers played. I liked the shift to that masculine energy after being with "the girls" all day and that mousy boss.

Buddy finally noticed me hanging out at the field, watching his games. I had waited, not patiently, for the day this might happen. Buddy had a notable record as an athlete at Savannah High, where he was three years ahead of me. The sparks began immediately. He appeared to be the tonic that I needed to get over the grief brought on by Joe (who is not worth any space in this narrative) the hot-blooded, slimy, macho jerk that had left me bereft with his faithless ways just months before.

My days at the bank went quickly, since I could spend time between customers thinking of the night when I would watch Buddy and his amazing pitching and batting skills on the field. This wonderland of new love and heated energy went on for several months.

Mama seldom made any comments about my choices in the love department but, for some reason, she made a point of having one of her famous coded message talks with me: "You know Buddy comes from that strong Baptist Church background and they do not approve of girls who smoke and drink." Mama had never talked to me about either of these issues. I did not smoke at home and apparently she did not know that my drinking ceased the day I threw up in Jay's car after drinking Salty Dogs at the beach. After that disgusting scene, I "got it"—drinking will make a mess. What Mama did not know was that Buddy smoked also. Besides, I had a much better idea of what he liked; Mayme did not need to tell me about that, a subject we would never broach.

The luster of this love affair began to wear off after about one year. Buddy lacked the ambition needed to rise above the world of blue-collar workers on the Savannah River. Even though I had always lived in that same world, the longing for glamour, adventure and anything, except "this," took over. I had no words to match this longing; just awareness that there must be another choice.

Buddy would talk about dreams of seeing the world, traveling, and living a different life. But I knew this would never happen; he used those same words when he talked about the life he would have liked as a professional athlete. He was a dreamer and a good man, just not "Mr. Right." Yet, at this point, I had no illusions about finding some dream guy; my track record proved that I only attracted losers.

One night we went so far as to start across the river into South Carolina where instant marriages were done. Halfway across the bridge, I said, "Let's wait and give more thought to this." Those words saved my life—so simple, so close to disaster. That night has played on my internal screen, over and over. I have a friend who describes her life as "a series of near misses." I shudder every time I think of that night and how close I came to major disaster.

Smooth landing, Chris, no bus in sight.

Longing and wishing continued—words began to take shape. At age nineteen, I could name what I wanted. "One day," I said to Buddy's sister, "I hope to meet an older man who has his act together. I am sick of immature, going-nowhere guys."

Ask and you shall receive.

******

I meandered around New Mexico and then crossed into Arizona. My destination was Edwards Air Force Base, California where Greg, my only child, now lived with his family. Memories from the 1960's, when we lived in Tucson, where Greg had his first birthday, rose with intensity as I pushed the van beyond the speed limit. Contrast that image with the reality that the very next day would be spent with my granddaughter, Elizabeth, for her second birthday. During the past year, I had seen her several times, but our brief visits never quite filled the cavern of longing to touch and hold her, a sensation that I felt daily.

The day of her birth in Pensacola, Florida, Greg brought her out of the delivery room with a loud exclamation, "Does anyone want to meet Elizabeth?" Yes, I wanted to meet Elizabeth, then and now. Instead of the gulf coast of Florida, we would meet in the California desert where the space shuttle sometimes landed and where test pilots have broken sound barriers. Greg had finished the second grade in California. Now he was a Captain and the father of a toddler. Old images mixed with new thoughts and wonderings about how this family scene might play out. Everything felt strange and, at the same time, had a bit of a familiar ring.

The western part of the country felt more like my real home than Georgia or Florida ever had. All together, we had spent eight years in Arizona, California and Washington State. My years in the clothing business had brought me to market in Los Angeles at least once each year. I knew the territory and yet driving out west alone felt strange. My mind kept flipping back and forth—then, now—then, now—I could not stay put.

My urge to visit another bizarre sight overtook me when I saw a sign pointing to Lake Havasu. The London Bridge was now situated there; piece by piece the entire span had been dismantled in London and shipped to Arizona. I entertained myself with images of the Chamber of Commerce brainstorming about plans to bring tourists to the area, when one of the advertising executives proposes the idea to buy the London Bridge—sure, Goofy.

London Bridge is falling down, falling down, my fair lady.

Visions of jumping rope on Brady Street to that refrain made me laugh out loud. I loved getting those old home movies on my private screen. Visiting London Bridge in the middle of this desert—how strange can that be?

Lake Havasu was created to bring power to Arizona by damming the Colorado River.

I want a water source to bring power to my dammed up soul. Maybe I could import a bridge to get me over to the other side of my messed up life.

The structure looked as though some deranged giant had just dropped it in a most unlikely spot.

I know that feeling of being plopped down where I do not belong. The sanity patrol could be watching you—who cares? This is my vehicle and I can think and do anything I please.

Well, not anything. I heard Mac warning me, "How fast are you going? If you don't control that heavy foot, you are going to get caught. It'll cost you!" Try as I might, I could not leave him behind. I had harbored a thought that Mac might surprise me by showing up in California. When I first planned the two-month trek, that image was in the mix; I told no one and certainly would not dare to suggest it to him. I wanted the thought to come out of some awakening of his own and not because I planted it. Alas, it would not be.

In retrospect, I know that if Mac had appeared, the focus of the pilgrimage would have been altered. Like one more piece of colored glass newly added to a kaleidoscope, his presence would have shifted my focus—even if I had no particular focus and no clue about why I happened to be there.

The spirit who made this plan knew how to keep me on the path.

The Escape

ALWAYS BE ON THE LOOKOUT FOR THE PRESENCE OF WONDER.

E.B. WHITE

IN JANUARY 1957, JUST A few days after my twentieth birthday, almost three years out of high school and still living with my parents, the "great escape" commenced. The phone call came. Mac on the other end reminded me that we had met from across the ledge of my teller's cage. He said I had been cashing checks for him for over a year, but no image of this man came up on my cognitive screen. Obviously, he had done some research on me; at least enough to get my name and home phone number.

I was entertained by his wacky chatter, and could not resist his tenacious charm, so I agreed to a date the next evening. Meanwhile, I planned to check out his marital status in the bank files. Many of the joint-checking types had tried to get me to meet them after work. I was never that desperate for a man. My search revealed that only his name appeared on his bank account—passed the first test.

That evening when he came to the door to pick me up, his face did not look at all familiar. He had not caught my eye in the bank. My days were filled with long lines of handsome men in uniform and they were mostly "business as usual" customers, not heart throbs. I saw him merely as one of the pack, but I kept that assessment to myself.

That first evening with him almost, instantly, put me under his spell. I had never met a man like him. The warm glow that had started with a phone call quickly became a bonfire.

I learned that this Lieutenant would soon pin on his new rank of Captain. He also had orders for Paris in the spring, just after his twenty-ninth birthday.

What have the gods dropped in my lap?

We saw each other every night. He would protest when I would say, "I need to get some sleep tonight. I can barely stay awake on the job and might fall off that tall stool." Miraculously, I would spring back to life in the evening, and except for the nights when he had a flight, we were out on the town.

His bizarre and goofy ways entertained me. Sometimes he would grab me while we were walking down the street, plant a juicy kiss on my lips and then start staggering off as if drunk. Other times, he might just break into a song and spin me around as though we were performers in a musical. These antics were mixed with a worldliness I had never encountered. He brought pieces that I was convinced my own life lacked—intelligence and fun—what more could a girl want?

Can I possibly keep up with this man? Would he tire of simple, uneducated me? He stunned me when he said he thought I had a good mind; no one since Mrs. Cobb, my first-grade teacher, had ever said anything so affirming to me. What did he base that on? It must have been something hidden that only he could see. Just the thought of how those words registered in my psyche still brings tears to my eyes. He saw a different *me* than the one I had previously thought was me—the woman who, above all, needed to look good.

Can I become this person he thinks I am? How do I go about that?

Three months passed quickly. On the day I had to say goodbye to my lover at the Savannah airport, I had no clue if this was the end of the affair, or if we had something lasting. The word marriage had come up, but Mac always qualified his remarks by adding, "You are so young. I want to give you some time to think about it." I had no visible sign of an engagement—no ring on my finger, and certainly nothing in writing about his intent.

I stood sobbing in the terminal as he lifted off the ground.

The first letter from Paris told me about the requirements for us to be married there. Upon arrival he had immediately stopped off at the legal office—so much for "time to think." The dream began to take shape—first, a place for us to live. He would start the search. I could not even create a picture of myself in Paris. I could pull up only an image of the Eiffel Tower, not the vaguest idea of how an apartment or house would look. Mac instructed me to get a passport and a legal document saying I had my parent's permission to marry. How outrageous, I thought I was all grown up.

My normal way to cope in any situation where my stupidity might show is to act as though I do this sort of thing everyday. I am a skilled performer on that particular stage. I concentrated on the wardrobe. Bank work occupied my days;

my nights were consumed with fantasizing about what awaited me on the other side of the world—far, far from Georgia.

Mama's worst fear, although she had never voiced it, was that I would end up carrying the baby of some no-good white trash. That day I left for Paris with a flat belly to marry Mac had to be the day her burden lifted. Most of my high school friends were already married and had kids, many of these babies had been delivered much sooner than the required nine months. I had managed to dodge that bullet, an entrenched tradition of my locale and our economic situation.

In all my twenty years, I had rarely crossed the line out of Georgia, never had been on an airplane, and could not have been more ignorant and unsophisticated about the outside world. But my black sheath with a black and white-checked duster, *haute couture* in the summer of 1957, kind of a Grace Kelly look, gave me all the confidence needed for the crossing—I looked good!

Mac told me in later years that he had seen me several times in the bank and I had caught his eye. However, he did not approach me until the day after he saw me walking out to my boss's car at the end of the workday. He said, "I needed to be sure the bottom half looked as good as the top half I had seen over the teller's cage." We were a perfect fit standing in the shallow end of the pool.

For a wedding gift, my folks promised to pay off my charge accounts. I had bought two outfits: first a dress to be married in with a striking little hat-type veil done in rose color lace with tulle overlay. The second was a suit made of blue gabardine and a handmade hat to match. The skirts of both accented my slim hips—I had to be careful about my weight to get the most mileage out of the style. This was, no doubt, the most important experience in my life. Truth be known, it was my only focus.

I then found the set of matching luggage to go with the perfect outfits. Like Mama, I had few skills for budgeting; the need to create an image guided me. On the day of the flight, the extra weight of my fully-packed, new luggage took forty dollars from my wallet, which left it almost as flat as its contents—a five-dollar bill.

Mama had gathered a crowd to send me off. She had all the skills for setting the stage, giving me my one and only moment in the spotlight. Even though I had not a clue about what awaited me on the other side of the Atlantic, every fiber of my being wanted liberation from what and where I had been. I waved goodbye to the crowd like Queen Elizabeth acknowledging her subjects—not a tear was shed as I lifted off the swampy Savannah soil.

When I arrived in New York, the agent at the Pan Am desk told me that the flight had been delayed; I would not leave until the next morning. I put on my "I can handle this" face, and said, "I will just wait right here." "You do not want to do that," she said. "We will pay for a taxi, a room and dinner for you." She gave me vouchers and directed me to the taxi stand. I spent the night in the famous Forest Hills Inn. What did I know of the place where famous tennis matches were held? Nothing!

I spent my few dollars to buy cigarettes, which I had given up since dating Mac, who had never smoked. I also bought a trash romance magazine and stayed awake all night reading graphic descriptions of what had been missing in my life since Mac left the country. Even these steamy stories could not keep me from worrying that I might sleep through the wake-up call.

I left the hotel long before I needed to, skipped breakfast and just went to the airport. Again, I tried to look as if I did this everyday.

Never let your history show.

I watched folks going by and tried my best to fit in with all the foreign-looking people. I did not call my family to tell them of my delay. It never occurred to me that they might expect a telegram from us when I arrived in Paris, expecting that Mac could take care of those details. I trusted him, my Captain.

When the flight finally left New York, I was one of only three passengers. August ended the tourist season—they were all coming home, not traveling east like me. The flight steward, Tony, sat with me most of the time and tried to talk me out of my marriage plan. "Go to Rome with me," he said, "we can have a real good time." He was darkly handsome and I figured Rome would be interesting, but Mac seemed like the sure bet. Life in the low country dissolved easily.

We touched down in Paris in the wee hours of the morning. Mac greeted me at Orly Airport in his usual wacky fashion, this time speaking French with a pronounced southern drawl—"*voulez vous coucher avec moi?*" he bellowed loud enough for all to hear. In 1957, living together had not been invented (at least not in my world), but what the heck, I was in France, the land of expatriates and Bohemian artists, and I was finally free. Plus, I needed to go to bed; I had not slept in days.

You bet, I'll sleep with you—take me there. This is really a graceful landing.

We walked into our sparsely furnished apartment on the third floor. Despite exhaustion, my mind started clicking off all the things we could do to make our space more pleasing to the eye. The living room/dining room and the master bedroom had floor-to-ceiling windows that could have made the place dramatic, however, the furnishings were just plain ugly. The view from the windows on one side looked like bombed-out ruins and, rising from the debris, there was an abandoned, partially-finished, five-story apartment building. Our building also had a not quite completed look, but at least it was habitable. I do not know what I expected, but this was not even close to my fantasies.

Next time, I choose where we will live.

The kitchen had a funny looking stove with two burners, and a tiny oven about one foot wide. I had few kitchen skills, so this did not bother me. The bathroom, however, was quite large with the toilet in a little enclosure; the fixture next to the tub caught my eye, a toilet-type thing with no seat on it.

"Is that another toilet?" I asked.

Mac howled, "That is a bidet."

"What is it for?"

"Think about it," he said. "You can figure it out."

Lordy, I have so much to learn, this place is strange.

Mac was not strange to me; I loved waking up in bed next to his hot body. I can still taste and smell the sweetness of that morning, so far from Savannah. I had come home, to my real home—not a dream, yet it felt filmy, as though I had stepped through a veil. Who ever would have imagined my escape would come by way of a sophisticated, handsome, great lover in Paris? And, he can pilot an airplane too—imagine that!

It seemed the French were in no hurry to do anything. Processing the paperwork for us to get married went into their low priority file. We found ourselves shuffled from one bureau to the next. Anxiety began to build for both of us—

maybe the French will never let us make this thing legitimate. Our families would not like this foreign way of sharing living quarters. Mama had told people I had a room in the home of friends of Mac's. I should have known Mama could invent any story she pleased. I found out years later that she had conjured up the entire announcement in the Savannah paper of my brother Hap's marriage. He got married in New Orleans and the only thing Mama knew about the bride was her first name. The rest of the information came from Mayme's great storehouse of fantasy names. She had given Millie a last name, a family, and a hometown, without a clue as to the facts.

Meanwhile, I lived in my own fantasy world in our apartment in *Choisy le Roi*, and daily fell more in love with everything French—the coffee, the patisserie, real butter, such a change from my margarine family.

Mac delighted in showing me the town, sitting in a sidewalk café and staring at each other, giggling about the wonder of it all. He told me over and over how difficult being alone had been for him over these past three months. He said he took lots of razzing from the guys in his squadron: "What in the world would cause a guy to transport a woman to Paris—look around, are you blind? It's like bringing ice to Eskimos."

At the same time I was being analyzed by the men in the Flight Service Squadron, I started my study of Paris and the French. Mac and I would go off on daily adventures. I loved having no destination, just being lost in the land of romance. The thought of those days still makes my heart race. On one of those treks, I discovered the bookstalls on the Seine—Henry Miller's books, banned in the U.S., were a stunning find. I could not believe some of those words were actually in print. The x-rated books all had green covers. The stack of books by my bed, indeed, quite quickly turned green.

I devoured the lusty, earthy words and messages. What an education!—another step in my liberation from the prison of my history.

Our wedding day finally came, thanks to an elderly American man who owned the hotel where Mac had lived before my arrival. We asked him to go with us and see if he could uncover what was delaying the processing of our paper work. I watched him pass a few French Francs over the counter to the clerk—so that's how you do it. *Voila!* The finished paper work magically appeared.

We were married the next day, with Mr. Worley and his even more elderly brother-in-law as our two witnesses. The brother-in-law spoke not a word of English. The four of us met outside City Hall. We walked into a room filled with very elegantly-dressed French people, all there to witness the marriage of the couple that followed us on the schedule. Since we had not invited anyone else to join us for the ceremony, I felt lucky to have such an impressive, well-dressed group present as we stood before the mayor and agreed to everything he asked of us.

Each time the mayor paused and looked at me, I said "*oui.*" Mac, over the years, would use this as leverage to get me to agree to whatever he wanted me to do. He would say, "You promised the mayor you would do this."

Thus began the "Pleasing Mac" era of my life—no doubt he knew what was best for both of us. As the "good wife" I fell into step, a respectful distance behind him.

******

As I crossed the border into California out of Arizona, anxiety overwhelmed me. In a few hours, I would arrive at

Edwards Air Force Base at the home of Captain Charles
Gregory McMillan, my only child.

> *That sounds so strange— my baby boy is a man. I
> remember when his daddy was an Air Force
> Captain. Where did those years go? It all happened
> so fast. Now there is Kelly in the picture and that
> precious baby, Elizabeth. Lord, I must be crazy to
> doubt whether or not I can be present with folks I
> love. What is wrong with me?*

The three weeks since I had left Quincy had huge blocks
of silence and my only conversations were with strangers. My
thoughts bounced all over the place as I tried to picture how
I might fill my role of mother and grandmother and feel at
home on a military base. Driving across this California desert,
demons of doubt assaulted me.

> *Get a grip, Chris. What possible problem could you
> have about just normal life in a house with your
> family? Slow down—quit looking for problems
> where none exist. And, why are you sweating and
> gripping the wheel?*

Greg surely had his own questions. He, no doubt, had
fears about his parents and the possibility of plans for a
divorce. I could imagine that my traveling alone plan might
cause him to wonder as to what in the hell was going on. I had
no pat answer to offer. If he were to quiz me, my words would
only add to the confusion, but nevertheless I began to practice
my defense.

> *The last year has felt as though I am pushing a
> boulder up a mountain and daily losing strength
> for the task. That sounds so stupid! Okay, maybe tell
> him about this contemplative life thing—convents,
> monasteries—oh forget it, you will really sound like*

*you need to be locked up. Just tell them, you love
them and that this pilgrimage is something you just
have to do.*

When I arrived at the guarded gate to the base, showed
my ID card that proved I was the wife of a retired officer,
entrance was quickly granted. I found their quarters easily. The
sight of Elizabeth, on the eve of her second birthday, put all
my fears to rest. What an amazing creature she was, verbal
far beyond her two years. She had no questions about why I
happened to be there without Papa. Just the touch of her soft
baby skin brought a blanket of comfort over my being.

Anxiety subsided and no third degree questioning
happened—relief. I felt peace and the pleasure of just being
with my family. Even that ubiquitous noise of their TV did not
cause distress.

*This is normal life, see, I know how to do it just as I
always have. I have not changed. I think I can, I
think I can, I know I can.*

The next day Elizabeth and I went to the base post
office. There she found a cross bar to sit on under one of the
tall tables, where she was soon joined by another little girl.
Elizabeth glanced at her and said, "What you name?" After
the child responded, Elizabeth pointed up at me and said,
"She name Gran." I wanted to just sit on the floor with them
and see if their perspective from under a table might help me
to get oriented—to know that "I be Gran."

*Do I be Gran? Has my old skin fallen away and a
new identity become visible that can only be seen by
a two-year-old? Is this the new me I set out to find
on this cross-country scavenger hunt? Can I bury the
businesswoman that stayed in constant motion, and
let Gran take over the body? God, who am I really?*

After a few days of contentment of just being Gran, I left the "happy home" scene and drove over to the coast to pick up my friend Vivian. She and I had a long-time relationship spanning our years as Air Force wives in Omaha. I also had spent time with her on my frequent buying trips to the Los Angeles Apparel Mart.

We planned a drive up through California and into Oregon. This rugged west coast had long ago taken the spot in my imagination as the place I would *go* when I died—my image of the perfect "eternal resting place."

This time I did not expect to leave my body in Big Sur, but I certainly carried plenty of baggage that I would like to toss over the edge and let drift out to sea. At the same time, I also knew I had not finished the time with my family and that I would return to Edwards in a few days. Doubts lingered about the unasked questions stored in our closets.

Stop it, Chris! Just look at that sunset over the water, be quiet—breathe.

Paris 1957

WE WERE THE ONLY AMERICANS in our apartment building. I would hale my neighbors with a "*bon jour*" or a "*bon soir*" as I passed them in the stairwell with my groceries stuffed in a little string bag, carried just like the locals. Though everything about my new home was unfamiliar to me, I gave it my best shot to look as though I knew "the ways" of the place.

I quickly learned that I had no aptitude for language. Truth be told, I did not take language study seriously. I managed to get along just fine without learning how to apply that senseless gender rule. Who decided that beer was feminine? What makes a book masculine? I did not know much, but for certain I knew "beer and book" were genderless. And besides, my South Georgia "ear" could not hear the subtle differences in certain sounds. My tongue failed me when I tried to say *monsieur*, it came out sounding more like *me sure*. In contrast, Mac took to the language like a native—my guy!

Our new friend Phillip, a French man who lived above us, seemed to enjoy a little chat each time we met; maybe he needed the opportunity to perfect his English. He often became the exact resource that I needed when I had to deal with any problem in the apartment.

This came in handy when I accidentally put my foot through the large window pane beside our bed sending glass spilling all over the parking area three floors below. I am sure we were the talk of the building. Phillip did not want to hear the details when we went to see him about finding the right person to call for repairs. His version of what might be happening in our bed, I am sure, was far more exciting than the fact that I merely stood on the bed and tried to step over Mac seemingly engrossed in a book. He looked up while I was mid-step above him and had one of his frequent moments of foolish thought. He grabbed the leg of my pajamas and sent me flying head down, feet up, as I kicked the glass wall.

Phillip always had this little sheepish grin whenever we saw him after our failed attempt to tell the story. He never learned the truth.

My greatest challenge presented itself with membership in the Officers' Wives Club which proved to be far more difficult than navigating the *marchés* in Paris. There were rules that my Georgia lower-class background could not comprehend. Entrée into this exclusive circle required that I step up my skills for "faking it." Those women were tough, but so was I. Fitting in with "the Wives" required more effort than speaking "marketplace French" and, in many ways, made less sense.

I had taken Bridge lessons at the YWCA in Savannah in preparation for my upcoming marriage. Those lessons paid off. The game of Bridge became my key to acceptance in the hat-gloves-rank-conscious world of older women. The Wives took me on as a project, bringing me along in the way they wanted me to go in order that I would become the "good spouse"—a proper "officer's wife." With my advanced skills for social deception, I managed to fit in at tea and cocktail parties.

With no thought of my missing competency, I invited a few of the high-ranking officer's wives to a luncheon at our apartment. With my usual naiveté, I planned a menu from the one cookbook that I had owned. Years later, my sister Frances told me how upset she was when I wrote home and told the family of my plan. She knew I had no cooking or entertaining experience, and certainly not with "important people" in my home. She feared that my childish attempt would do damage to Mac's career. I had no idea what my guests thought of my pitiful attempt at entertaining. Awareness of my sister's doubts caused me to ponder and then laugh out loud about how silly I must have looked.

Mac, to his great credit, never put any pressure on me to be anything other than my natural self. He never believed in a required social life. He was one of the few officers I'd known who did not drink, not even wine. There we were in the land of grapes and vineyards and neither of us imbibed. Many years later, I have more than made up for my earlier asceticism.

Our teetotaling habits made us strange creatures in the cocktail party environment of the military. Our best friends, Kay and Winn, consumed our share. Most parties at the Officers' Club ended with one of us driving their car home and seeing to it that they stayed there. We spent many weekends with them, watching them get knee-walking drunk. They loved us and we loved them. They were bright, interesting people who just happened to be addicted to strong spirits.

Anytime Mac could take leave time, we traveled—that was our addiction. In January of 1958, we went to the Riviera, Monaco, and then Switzerland. As we drove through the breathtaking scenery of the Alps, I saw snow for the very first time in my life. At the first sighting, I asked Mac to stop and let me put my feet in the fluffy stuff. He pulled to the side of the road and without one thought as to the consequences of my eagerness for this new experience, I opened the door, jumped out, and slid under the car. Mac laughed so hard, he could not even inquire about the condition of my bones. Only my pride was hurt. I looked ridiculous crawling out from under the car. Another lesson learned.

Think before you jump off that curb, Chris.

That same year, I went with a friend to London. The streets were icy in spots, but I managed to keep my balance. Being with English speakers made the travel so easy, even if I did have to attune my ear to some disparity. My world expanded and, gradually, the lessons sunk in. I stayed upright and began to gain confidence.

In late 1958, we went to Brussels to The World's Fair where the Atomium was the centerpiece structure. The shiny, metal tinker-toy-looking piece represented the molecules in the atom. My limited understanding of the universe could not begin to comprehend the message.

On a recent change of flights in Brussels, I had a glimpse of the Atomium, and with that sighting what followed was a flood of memories.

Looking at the faces of all those people with their many skin colors and body shapes, I try to imagine what life might be like through their eyes. Then there is that DNA thing that is the same in all of us.

Brussels 1958—a Zen moment—"at one with the universe."

From Brussels, we drove to Amsterdam where Mac bought a two-carat diamond for my first anniversary present. Until that day, I had only a spindly little wedding band, visibly unimpressive. The new sparkling gem said volumes to me about who I had become in this first year. I finally felt valued.

The first night I wore the ring, I dreamed that I had lost it. I think of that dream often and believe it to be the precursor to the journey I would eventually take. I had to find my way to the place where I did not have to depend on a man to validate me or make me feel safe and secure. On that day in Amsterdam, I had no idea of what lay ahead; I just soaked up the sparkle as it sunk deeply into my being.

Wearing a two-carat diamond, or any size diamond, had never been a thought I'd entertained. Diamonds and fancy weddings meant nothing to me. Friends of mine seemed to do that sort of daydreaming; I only knew some possibility existed outside the lines that confined or defined me. Picturing such a life was not easy, since there were no role models in my early life. I had to depend on the inventive genes that I'd inherited from Mama. Living in Paris, traveling in Europe, certainly had never played on my internal screen. Each day started with a blank page and I wrote the words on it as they came to me from some unknown source.

I think about a friend whose young son heard him singing a silly song and said to him, "Daddy, whoever wrote that song made it up." I did not write the script for my life, I only read the lines and stood on the footprints marked for me. Whoever wrote my script definitely made it up.

When exposure to "good literature" came into my life, I know my dial had to be pre-set. Before life in Paris, I had never been around anyone who read or discussed books. I listened when others mentioned something interesting that they had read or were reading, made note of it, and immediately found the book.

My choice of reading material only included novels, never non-fiction. Mac, across the room or the bed, read a dictionary or history book. I shared space with a human being who in most every way made odd choices—certainly odd to my way of seeing. I liked stories, Mac preferred "just the facts." I benefited from his storehouse of knowledge, and he seemed to gladly take on the role of teacher.

One day I said, "We need washing powder the next time you go to the store on base." He fell over laughing and said, "Washing powder? You are not in the backwoods of Georgia anymore!" He always had a lesson plan, all I had to do was pay attention and listen to the instructions. To this day, I can hear his voice telling me how much he loved the sound of a certain word. He looked up from his dictionary and with all seriousness said, "I love the *P* words, like perspicacious and penurious." No kidding—what a guy! I had never heard either of those words nor have I ever forgotten them.

Occasionally, I did get a little glimpse into the tests that were coming my way while we lived our fairytale life. Mac was a good friend, a great lover, fun and nutty. But, after a while, a dark shadow began creeping in. He, most of all, needed to be in control. After all, he was the Captain, a college graduate, and a pilot. I had no leverage. I could not match his gift for language or compete with his bank balance and the armor that protected it from my careless ways. He handled the money, thus felt he wielded all the power. I despised the feeling of being "on the dole," and we had huge fights about my need to work out a more equitable system.

Mac did not believe in joint checking accounts. Marriage, to him, seemed to be only about sharing a bed not a checkbook. He had the language to work out equality in the bedroom but not in the office. I had far to go before I could find my way through this rough terrain. Despite the arguments, this little flaw seemed minor and it did not cause too much distress.

As I aged or, "grew up," the money deal brought out my fierce warrior woman personality. I found my footing on a new battlefield and, for the first time, saw the chinks in Mac's armor. In later years, he would describe me by saying, "She is not the woman I married."

You got that right, Bud, she's not.

******

Vivian, a soul sister for over 20 years, seemed to fit perfectly into my plan for the next leg of my pilgrimage. She and I had met during the late 60's; we were fellow seekers of the time, a period of great transition for our country and for many of us. The time with Greg and family had made me wonder how I might deal with sharing time with anyone else, especially Vivian, since our pattern always consisted of hashing over every thought and every detail of our lives—silence never occurred when we were together. The awareness that our "talking time" would help me to sort out the thoughts that had come since I'd left home made me eager to have her company.

We spent a couple of days in San Francisco, and then drove up the coast through the giant redwood forest and into Oregon. Vivian had made reservations for us in a retreat center that neither of us knew anything about except for the fact that we had read the books of the founder. We arrived there in the early afternoon. The minute we walked in, Vivian said, "I do not like this place, it feels like a hospital."

"No," I countered, "it's fine, you'll see. It's just that antiseptic smell. I think they have a hot tub and a massage room. The place certainly looks clean."

"It looks like a damn hospital, I do not like the feel of it," she said in rebuttal.

I ignored her negative comments and just chalked them up to her frequent ways of finding fault that I'd labeled as her "critical mother voice." We put our things in the room. Still, Vivian looked like she was seeing ghosts at every turn. "Let's go for a walk and when you see the neighborhood, you will feel better," I promised. Vivian walked beside me and spoke not one word. When we came back to the center, I stopped in the kitchen to talk with the group preparing our dinner. After two minutes of that scene, I went back to the room where Vivian sat on the side of the bed looking as though she might have a seizure.

"Get your stuff and let's get out of here," I said. Vivian, being a slow processor, never reacted quickly. I was always waiting for her to catch up. This time she had her suitcase and purse and was flying, like a terrified hummingbird, out to the van.

As we pulled away, she said, "What happened in the kitchen?" "Those people have been brainwashed," I replied. "They are unable to respond to a simple question, like 'What are we having for dinner?'" Instead, they chanted in unison words from their leader about the meaning of life. I assured her, "Your vibes were right, but I think it is an asylum, not a hospital."

We both started laughing uncontrollably. We laughed all the way to the liquor store where we bought the best bottle of wine we could find and then found a motel with a great view. To this day, we have no idea what that place was all about and what was going on there. Interestingly enough, one book written by the founder had the words "conscious living" in the title. Either the residents of his establishment did not grasp the concept of consciousness or maybe we didn't. We did not hang around to find an answer, nor did we drink their Kool-Aid.

From there, we crossed the mountains toward the center of the state and spent two nights in Canyonville, where Vivian's aunt and uncle lived just off the interstate. The couple, well into their eighties, had no indoor plumbing. We stayed in a motel down the road where, thankfully, we had a flush toilet and shower. Watching these two free spirits, really old hippies, function in their tiny space, where plates from every state in the union decorated the walls, could now go on my list of extraordinary places worth visiting.

Vivian's aunt's name was "Mexia" which rhymed with "Texia"—Vivian's mother's name. Mexia had migrated from Texas when she was a young girl and there met and married Lawson, a northwestern frontier, storytelling character. Together they ran a little café in their home. When the state began building the interstate within a few yards of their front door, they fought a winning battle to get an exit that would bring even more business to their two-table establishment. This woman could make a pie people would drive for miles to buy. They invited a houseful of local, quite-colorful characters to come and meet us. We feasted on Lawson's hamburgers and Mexia's pie while stories filled the air. This day, alone, would have been enough to make my cross-country trip worthwhile.

My favorite quote from Lawson was, "I planned to read the Bible all the way through, but I got busy picking prunes and never did get to it." I think of him often when I realize something has distracted me from what I had set out to do, like in the midst of gathering tax info, I decide to wash my car. I imagine Lawson found picking prunes much more engaging than reading the Bible. His stories were far better than those found in the book of Judges or Chronicles. One day, I might make a plaque with his words on it for my wall. Some of my fundamentalist friends might think I am being irreverent. I am.

We left there with the glow of Mexia and Lawson still lingering about us. I dropped Vivian off at her home in Lompoc, California where fields of flowers grow that produce most of the seeds for the gardens in this country. I left that lush scene, and then drove across the barren desert back to Edwards Air Force Base and to my family. I wanted more time with them, especially Elizabeth, but in retrospect I know I wanted the return to solitude even more. The glut of words used in the past week was beginning to feel like an assault on my being.

After a couple of days of quiet time lost, my spirit went into convulsions. The mundane sounds of a household felt as though I had landed in a torture chamber. For two nights, no sleep came; I had to get away. The voices in my head screamed for me to run for my life. There were no words I could find to explain this need to flee, to be alone, and to sort out the mass of unresolved emotional chaos that had sent me out originally. Greg and Kelly appeared confused when they awoke and found me ready to leave sooner than they had expected. I could not make sense of it, and they certainly could not. If I had tried to tell them, I'm certain it would have convinced them I needed to be locked up for my own safety and for the good of all.

Mama is just not rational.

As I drove across the Mojave Desert and started the trek back east, I was aware that this turnaround moment was my breaking point. I had no idea what caused me to snap, but snap I had.

Lord, help me. I am a mess, one screwed up, out of control, poor excuse for a human being. Surely this will send Mac out here to rescue me.

Birthing

THE REAL VOYAGE OF DISCOVERY CONSISTS NOT IN
SEEING NEW LANDSCAPES BUT IN HAVING NEW EYES.

MARCEL PROUST

AFTER A YEAR IN MY wonderland of entertaining high ranking people, gathering with The Wives, going to Paris cafes, etc., I got pregnant and my world began to twist sideways. In 1958, there seemed to be a law sent down from the "big guy" up there, etched in stone: *woman shall not gain one ounce more than twenty pounds in this nine-month period.* The world controlled by men from above and below was cruel and unyielding and even though I had supposedly come of age, now a grown up twenty-one-year-old woman, I felt as though I had no say in this matter of my bodily changes.

Everyday, the torture began with morning sickness. When that misery subsided, raging hunger took control. Pounds began to stack up like Gran's hoecakes. I consumed every morsel of food with full awareness that a doctor, my commanding officer husband, and The Wives. who bought into this male-made dictum, were monitoring every bite I ingested. They became both judge and jury. I had no defense; I *was* guilty. When they were not on their soapboxes looking down at me, the voice in my head screamed even louder words of condemnation.

I had planned the pregnancy. I wanted this baby and everything about my condition felt right, except for the straightjacket these "dear persons" tried to keep me in. The Wives seemed not to care in the least what I might be feeling—bitches! They offered no sympathy, just harsh rules and precise measurement of what I should eat. I felt like a criminal stealing little bites when no one was looking.

If I did go to a luncheon or bridge club, I became the main attraction. They had taken me on as a "class" project when I first arrived, and now the work intensified as my waistline expanded. My feeding and its visible results became the focus every time we gathered.

The night I liberated myself from this hell-on-earth "courtroom" was a scene that I still recall in vivid detail. A group of four couples had dinner with the squadron commander and his wife at their home in the Paris suburbs. We were seated at their very European looking, elongated, dining table; me at one end and Mac at the other. After dinner, during a lively gambling board game, the hostess brought out a new supply of snacks and unfortunately placed a tray of chips next to me. I automatically reached for a few and just as I started to put the first salty, crunchy tidbit in my mouth, Mac, in his most commanding voice, said, "You're not going to eat those are you?" My "fight or flight" instinct took over without a single thought as to the consequences of the action. The chips flew to his end of the table and I coolly said, "**No**."

The room came to a complete halt with a painfully silent, *pregnant* pause. The "real" me had been exposed: trashy upbringing, uncouth, no discipline, a bad wife and, for sure, not fit to raise a child. I do not recall feeling embarrassed. I was furious and knew I had reached the end of my tolerance for the lot of them. I felt only rage and wanted to flee.

Who put them in charge of me? Damn bossy know-it-all bunch.

That night, my life took a dramatic turn. I have not thrown food since, but never again have I blindly succumbed to ridiculous rules, most especially those about my *very own* body.

Mac did not speak to me for two days. He became the bus that hit me and then backed up over me to complete the kill. I sat next to him in icy silence on Thanksgiving Day at the Officer's Club. No one at our table had any comment about my diet. For that part of the silent treatment, I gave thanks. It was a painful test, but I felt as though I jumped another hurdle and landed on my feet, yet one more time. No one again brought up the subject of my weight.

In *Wild Geese*, Mary Oliver says it better than I ever could:

YOU DO NOT HAVE TO BE GOOD.
YOU DO NOT HAVE TO WALK ON YOUR KNEES
FOR A HUNDRED MILES THROUGH THE DESERT,
REPENTING.
YOU ONLY HAVE TO LET THE SOFT WARM ANIMAL OF
YOUR BODY LOVE WHAT IT LOVES.

Not a doubt about our love for each other—no question there, but lord, Mac and I had temperaments akin to oil and water—no blending. Soon after this major upset, our attention became focused on a change of location.

Mac's Flight Service Squadron had an office in Ankara, Turkey and his name came up as the person to fill a position. In my fifth month of gestating, we made the move. My doctor said, "You should not make the whole trip at one time." These instructions were so much kinder than the weight gain warning. Following those orders was easy. We spent three December days in Rome; I smile each time I recall the image of my pregnant body wearing a heavy tweed coat and standing in front of Saint Peter's in my high heel pumps. We had a grand time and I ate whatever I jolly well pleased and savored every moment of it.

We flew from Rome to Istanbul before continuing on to Ankara. An odor I could not identify greeted us as we walked into the terminal. My overly sensitive gag reflex started to kick in. I asked Mac if he recognized the unpleasant aroma. He said, "I don't know, but it smells like everyone here is wearing dirty socks." A little detective work led us to discover the source—a restaurant right next to the gate where we would depart for the last leg of our flight. The smell turned out to be food.

What has the military done to me? I want my French coffee, not this thick stuff served in thimble size cups. Where is my fresh baguette? How did I get to this place? Oh god, I can't stop gagging.

As we flew to Ankara, the disgusting odor seemed to follow. My olfactory senses could not escape the stench. We arrived in Ankara where the taxi driver understood Mac's instructions to take us to The Modern Palace. This hotel was neither of those things, but it became our home for two months in this capital city. Our room on the fifth floor caught all the odors wafting up from the kitchen. My eating binges ceased. The Wives and my doctor had failed, but Turkey succeeded in reining in my out-of-control diet. After a few weeks, my body adjusted and, to my astonishment, I discovered I actually loved this food laced with garlic and exotic spices. Lamb, which I had never eaten, became my favorite.

My days were spent in the hotel reading books like *War and Peace* and *Anna Karenina*. I fell in love with Russian literature while lounging in my dreary room. The military mission was to keep us safe from the evil ways of those communists just across the Black Sea from Turkey. I welcomed their literary giants into my chamber, and wondered what life might be like for these nearby neighbors. Folks who could write so elegantly could not be bad people.

Occasionally, I ventured out to the markets, but it seemed as though my pregnant body became a spectacle on the streets. Maybe if I had been veiled, I would not have been noticed. Somewhere, I had heard that in Turkey, unlike other Muslim countries, women did not wear the *hijab*, but this was certainly not true in the markets in Ankara. I saw the same number of covered women there as I did in many Islamic countries in later years.

I loved everything about being pregnant and even had the overfeeding problem under control. Anticipating birth felt like waiting for Christmas. I could not wait to unwrap this present growing inside my body. Without a doubt, this was a boy that I felt jumping around in my belly, probably a basketball player.

Our new home felt like the perfect place to give birth. It was not far from the Holy Land. Imagine that! The Blessed Virgin Mary and me? Of course, my child will be a boy. I sewed all my maternity clothes and continued to wear those skinny-heel pumps right up to the end. Looking good was still of utmost importance.

We moved into our stucco home in the suburbs just weeks before the due date. There, I first observed the daily ritual of Muslims stopping in the midst of the workday to put down prayer rugs to kneel for prayer (for the third time of the five required of every believer, every day of the week.) I loved the sight of city workers outside our house on their knees. *If only I could feel that kind of call to stop and seek the presence of the holy. These folks have something I want.*

During Ramadan, our landlord invited us to dinner at his home—after sunset, of course. All but pregnant women, sickly people, small children or frail elders were required to fast from early morning until sundown. When the only meal of the day is served, the table overflows with exotic dishes. My mind could not imagine having discipline enough to fast from sunrise to sunset, especially in my condition. In spite of our obvious differences, I felt at home in this foreign setting; it was a most hospitable place. Our host's wife spoke only Turkish, but this fact did not keep us from forming a fast friendship. Being "with child" connects women in that place beyond language and she brought gracious determination to forge this bond.

The minor discomforts that came with late stages of pregnancy did not distract me from my task of getting our house and nursery ready. Daily life was challenging, but adjusting to whatever came my way presented no insurmountable problem. I think I thrived in that environment and loved figuring out how to take care of the routine needs of the household. After all, I had survived life in my family's fifteen dollar-a-month rental house on Brady Street and, after that, in the housing project. I had a mission and met every challenge with my usual degree of arrogance. Turkish utilities, or the lack of them, did not slow me down. Drinking water was carried to the house in big jugs from the Base Exchange. Tap water had to be boiled and a few drops of Clorox added. Turkish bottled milk did not meet our standards; we had to substitute powdered milk.

Like Mayme, I had asked no questions about this birthing thing. I saw the doctor as required, took my vitamins, bought cloth diapers, and checked everything off my "to do" list. But, in truth, my act resembled Prissy in *Gone with the Wind*. Just like her, I thought, "I knew all about birthing babies." Doubts about my competency never came on my screen.

In 1959, husbands usually were banned from the labor room, but in this small facility in Ankara, this rule was suspended. I naively asked Mac to come in with me. In my mind, I could see the whole show. We would just hold hands and have an intimate, precious moment. We would be together until I had to go into the delivery room that was certainly off limits for men, unless they happened to be doctors. The scene had played in my mind many times and I never doubted this would be a special and a magical moment for us.

The night when the labor pains started to get spaced closer together, we grabbed my bag with nightgowns, toilet articles and the required diapers. I waddled into the hospital, where the nurses immediately took charge of my body and performed a few procedures that I will skip in this narrative.

Mac and I then settled into the closet-sized space called a labor room. For a short period we had some measure of civility until the helpless hell of body functions broke loose. Did I mention the enema? I dragged myself from the bed and hobbled to the bathroom until, finally, pain pinned me to the bed. I grabbed Mac and screamed "Make it stop! Why in the hell doesn't someone help me? I cannot do this." Those wise bitches, The Wives told me that labor hurt, but I was certain this present agony went way beyond normal labor pain. The scene got ugly in a hurry.

My god, this really hurts—make it stop! Please!
Please! Do something!

I have no idea what poor Mac witnessed beyond this point; I was barely conscious for the night. The script did not match the one I had rehearsed, and Mac was without one altogether. We were pathetic. He could not escape from the tiny cell and the screaming mad woman. I continued to frantically beg to be rescued—no one answered or even responded to my plea. Was I invisible?

After about 12 hours of this horror show, I heard a nurse yell for help to get me to the delivery room. In my semiconscious state, I saw the bloody mess between my legs as they lifted me onto a gurney. I had no idea there was hemorrhaging involved in this process—then thought "Oh god, poor Mac." Why did I not ask questions?

Damn you Mayme, you trained me too well.

I left the hospital a totally changed woman, but still unable to sort out the new reality flooding my consciousness. Twenty-two years old and only 18 months out of Georgia, nothing about me looked like the vain creature that had strutted onto that airplane in Savannah in her fashionable black-and-white outfit. It is hard for me to believe that some people actually pray for humility. Could they possibly know what horrifying life experience might bring them to their knees, to that moment of humiliating powerlessness? Moments such as this just happen and then, when it is over, maybe one can rise to the heights and say thanks for that slap in the face.

My loss of blood had been so severe that recovery did not occur quickly. Nothing about the experience looked the way I had pictured it. My physical weakness was minimal compared to the loss of my confidence.

Miss Scarlet, I don't know nothing bout birthing no babies!

I told Mac he would have to find a full time nurse. That baby boy would surely die if he had to depend on me for his survival. The Captain felt pretty helpless, too. What a mess we were.

I had thought having a baby live with us would be sort of like playing with a doll. I now had this person dependent on me to behave like a responsible grown-up. Holy shit, this was serious work! I had given birth to a *person* and not a "baby doll." He had a name—Charles Gregory McMillan—a real live human being with survival needs. My immature mind could not take in such a shocking fact.

All the other women around me seemed to know how to do this. I was convinced that only I had doubts about the mothering thing. Apparently god left out the "mother know how" connection when my parts were knit together. My experience of being parented offered little guidance. Mama and Daddy just seemed to let us grow up and they did almost nothing to help us in our process.

We had been the victims of castor oil for all our wellness needs. Anything that ailed us could be cured with that vile stuff which was followed by sucking on an orange. Since I came last in Mayme's brood, I had no idea how she mothered a newborn. My baby needed more than castor oil and an orange with a hole in it. There were only a few doctors in the little military clinic. Doctor Spock, the child-raising guru of the 50's, became my constant reference source. I kept him close by. He, along with a Canadian nurse who lived next door, became my lifelines. Nothing about being a mother felt natural, only scary.

This was my one and only birthing experience. What a teacher! When I look back on that ill-prepared child who gave birth to a son on April 12, 1959, I fluctuate between embarrassment and sorrow. I take responsibility for my lack of preparation, arrogance and ignorance. Then I feel the sadness for all women, my sisters, who lack guides to show them the way. Maybe we have all become wiser since 1959.

We returned to the States when Greg was seven-months-old. Mama had gathered a huge crowd at the Savannah airport to welcome us. Needless to say, the woman who exited on that ramp did not resemble the one who had left there in 1957. For the first time ever, I gave no thought to the clothes on my back.

After the royal welcome, we settled in with Mama and Daddy for a few days with Greg as our centerpiece. My fantasy about this family I had left behind was that we were a close-knit bunch. Wrong. We were people who asked no questions, and, as a result, we knew little of each other. In fact, clearly, we had no interest in getting to know the other. We only played the game of "kin." There was no intentional unkindness, only an emotional void, and a gaping chasm within and between each one of us. We all sat around and watched Greg do baby things.

On the other hand, Mac's family in Quincy, where we went next, asked lots of questions about our time in foreign places. His parents, three brothers and their families wanted facts about us. They gathered round the parents' home and told funny stories; some were of local girls who remained angry since I snagged the last McMillan brother. They loved to tell about all the broken hearts Mac had left in his wake when he flew off to Paris and then sent for me. We laughed and had fun. I loved this new family; they took me in. I gladly joined the McMillan Clan.

We soon moved to the west coast with vacations in Quincy every year. Greg had cousins; we had family. We visited Savannah too, but my feeling of distance from life there never changed. The pattern had been set early on; I managed to ignore the churning feeling in my gut and to play the part of the "good daughter." Savannah held dark memories and I had no desire to let a spotlight in. I wanted that door to remain closed. The courage to let any light into that basement room in my psyche came bit by tiny bit many years later.

Turn now—stay balanced—jump—nice landing— watch out for that bus.

******

The afternoon after my early morning, dramatic, sudden exit from Greg and family at Edwards Air Force Base, I checked into a motel in Kingman, Arizona. In a fit of hysteria, I called Mac. My mixed-up mind had led me to the mistaken notion that he knew of my morning madness and that he would be worried. I could not have been more wrong. My Prince Charming was not mounting the white horse and riding west to rescue me.

Just somebody please help me—would a call to 911 send someone charging in here to save my sorry-ass soul? This pain is more horrific than that day in the labor room in Ankara. Well at least, I'm not visibly bleeding this time.

I felt as though I was a drowning person watching my entire life played out for me in living color—a meaningless, dull, silly drama. There was no "and, they lived happily ever after" at the conclusion. There was no conclusion. The torture did not stop; I could not find the button to shut off this internal picture show.

Married all these years, yet so alone. I could not figure out how I had come to this rock bottom spot.

> *Where the hell is Kingman, Arizona, and why am I here of all places? Could this be what Scott Peck in The Road Less Traveled labeled as the final stage in maturing, the coming to terms with one's aloneness? This feels like shit—I don't want to be mature.* **Help!**

The motel walls gave back no answer. My inner critic was working overtime. She was digging around in and picking scabs off of old wounds, a bad habit started in my childhood. Mac had never been able to understand this aspect of my personality. I remember a conversation with him about some situation, and my search for a solution. I commented about the need to change our point of view; he replied, "If you think for one minute I am going to put myself through all that self-examination stuff you go through in order to come up with a new life philosophy; you're wrong! I refuse to look that deeply." He was a true conservative and New Thought did not interest him. He had his old answers and they worked well enough.

The only satisfactory conversations I had with him during my time on the road had to do with car maintenance. Mac, the pilot, was the expert in our family on mechanical stuff. Several times when I made emergency calls, he would brighten up and talk at length about what weight oil to get and the other inner workings of my vehicle. I wanted to talk about my own inner workings, but he had not been to special schools to learn how to translate my inarticulate melancholic search. Despite his facility for language, he could not comprehend what he thought of as my "mumbo-jumbo."

Agonizing over life was my job and I could do it well. On that night I was getting my Ph.D. in loss, grief and soul longing. My universe lacked any order. I was spinning out of control, totally alone with only a tiny thread to keep me anchored. I could not define that thread that kept me from walking out the door and stepping in front of the first truck on the exit ramp of Interstate 40. God knows the temptation was there, but underneath remained an awareness that I could never be so irresponsible as to leave those I love with the burden of the unresolved mess of my life. What misstep had I taken that landed me in this dark pit?

If I ever have the need to see or experience any feature of hell, Kingman, Arizona is the picture I pull up. Ghosts of my past taunted me. I saw the young child living on Brady Street, a child who hated everything about her life. All my judgments about my parents came back to haunt me—not a doubt. I saw clearly how I could have been more tolerant of the character flaws I saw in them.

I could have loved them instead of being such a harsh critic. My relationship with Mac could have been different, if only I could have found it in my emotional range to love more, to give more, to be more accepting. Shut up Saint Francis. Why could I not care more about loving and less about being loved? Why am I not out at Edwards making cookies with Elizabeth and acting like a normal grandmother? Surely, I am flawed to my core. **Help!**

My body and soul were being stretched to the breaking point. In the past, I had experienced some short episodes of depression, times of low energy, feelings of despair. What was expressed this time was not depression; this state of being had energy that ricocheted off the walls. The room had heat waves coming up from the cheap carpet. A pulse like a banging drum assaulted my mind.

Body and spirit came apart. There was no letup and certainly no sleep. Condemning voices assaulted me through the night. This pit was too deep, I had spent 54 years digging down deeper and deeper and there was no way out. The handsome Captain was not coming to save me. I had failed. There would be no second chance; I could not retake the test.

Sleep must have overtaken me at some point, but I have no memory of any relief from the agony. In spite of physical and emotional exhaustion, I was awake. I hoisted my limp body into the driver's seat and set out for the Grand Canyon where I had a room reserved. My only goal for the day was to focus on driving and arrive at the canyon before dark. The murky gloom of Kingman stayed with me as I clicked off the miles.

I distracted myself by trying to organize thoughts around a letter that I would write to Greg and Kelly. I knew there were no words that would make them understand this pilgrimage, yet I tried to string some together to satisfy my need to at least appear to be responsible. Mainly, I wanted them to know that they had not caused my breakdown; this inexplicable behavior was only about me. I could not explain my actions to myself and certainly lacked any capacity to convey my inner logic to them. This "dark night of the soul" stuff was not a topic in their range. I would not embarrass myself by trying to communicate any words about my inner workings, my emotional chaos of the moment. I knew they loved me and wished me well and I consoled myself with that thought. This letter would be better than nothing and at least give me some relief me from my guilt.

Nothing outside of my mind on the drive from Kingman to the Grand Canyon caught my attention. That terrain is totally missing from my memory bank. I could have been arrested for DUIM: driving under the influence of melancholy.

Lord, lord, will I ever get over my sorrow?

After a quick look at Flagstaff and their lunch pickins, I drove to the Canyon and another drab motel room with plastic seemingly outdoor furniture, crass art and a ghastly bedspread. With the sleazy bedspread safely stashed in a far corner, I set out to see the big hole in the ground. My good friend, Dan, had told me to remember that I could not fly when I got to the edge. I smiled when I thought of Dan. Without a doubt, my mind was flying; perhaps it would take my split-off body with it.

I had experienced this magnificent sight, years before, but this time felt different. There seemed to be some mission, something other than just following the guidebook that describes what one is supposed to see at the site. My body seemed to be pulled to the edge of the gorge by a magnetic force. It was late afternoon when I began my meditative walk and viewing around the border of the chasm. By the time the sun started to set, I no longer had awareness of tourists nearby. New words were being formed from a voice I did not recognize.

The streaks of light and shadows I witnessed that afternoon in the gorge were the best sermon I have ever heard; they spoke to me of the mix of light and dark in my life. My night of complete blackness made me identify with Jesus' time alone in the garden of Gethsemane. I could hear him saying to the sleeping disciples, "Can't you just stay awake and pray with me?" The message I began to hear told me that I had to face my solitary darkness and hang in there. There

was no other way to find the light. Jesus, too, wanted someone
to comfort and *be* with him as he faced the confusing void
and the invitation to embrace his own suffering. We are led to
believe that he knew what awaited him; I'm not convinced he
was so sure. His cry for help and companionship came from a
human who felt the agony of not knowing what was going to
happen next; only the terror of the moment existed. I hear in
that plea a man begging to be saved. Who can blame him for
wanting to be spared the next step in Matthew 26:39: "Lord,
if this cup may pass from my lips, please let it...." He had
only that inner voice, the same one that had been his guide
for all of his life. This glimpse of his agony revealed to me the
fullness of his humanity.

In the last light of that day, I saw the god I encountered
as a mirror of the god inside me, an inner guide. Some part
of me died in that motel room the night before and my
resurrection happened as a pinpoint of light appeared in my
dark interior. The moment was sensual. I felt the Arizona
landscape with my whole body—the wide-open spaces, the
big skies, the giant chasm in the earth, the colors of the sunset.
I then knew, without a doubt, that all those same atoms made
up my being.

The kingdom is within—where had I heard that?
Why had I not remembered it? How can this be
real? Nothing is different and yet everything has
changed.

My logical mind wanted a logical answer. It offered me
no place for such paradoxical thought to simply rest. Where
could I file it? The answer had to be *this* or *that*. How does
one adjust to living in the space between this and that? My
search for answers had brought me here to this huge hole in

the ground, this earth womb. Truth seemed to reside in the abyss.

My motel room that night housed none of the demons from the previous night in Kingman. Instead, there was only the roar of silence, the healing vibrations and that same pulse that I had detected at several stops along the journey since leaving home. The screaming, condemning voices became a soft lullaby. The planet kept revolving and evolving, the motion rocked me to sleep.

Out West

IT MAY BE THAT WHEN WE NO LONGER KNOW WHICH WAY
TO GO WE HAVE COME TO OUR REAL JOURNEY. THE MIND
THAT IS NOT BAFFLED IS NOT EMPLOYED. THE IMPEDED
STREAM IS THE ONE THAT SINGS.

WENDELL BERRY

IN 1960, MAC, GREG, AND I moved to Tucson. Mac had been in school to learn to fly KC 97s, the tankers that refuel other airplanes in mid-air—mainly the big bombers. Greg and I had stayed in Florida and Georgia most of that time, but there, in Tucson, we were a family again, reunited with our familiar household bits and pieces from Turkey.

We furnished the three-bedroom, ranch-style house on base with the latest trends of early American maple, mixed with the foreign treasures from Europe and Asia. Greg started walking just as we settled into our new quarters. Domestic bliss set in as I decorated and watched my baby boy take his first steps. In 1960, one year since his birth, I had discovered that I could actually rise to this mothering challenge. I amazed myself, what with the house, the baby and me? This was a stunning picture of perfection in my mind—sheer improvisation.

I polished Greg's white shoes each night. Diapers hung out each morning to dry along with Mac's khaki uniforms and the short shorts that were my uniform of the day. The McMillans radiated the happy family image of the new decade. Greg's playpen resided in the carport where the stroller also waited for our daily walks though the neighborhood. Greg splashed merrily in the baby pool in our backyard.

Never in my wildest dreams could I have thought up such a scene. Then a new yearning crept in, a longing for another baby took control of my thoughts and quickly became an obsession. Well-meaning friends counseled me about the harm that might come to Greg if he had to grow up as an "only child." He was so cute. No way could I stand back and let this happen. The haranguing voices told me that I could not rest until this family was made *completely* whole. I felt cajoled.

Another baby, that's all we need. This time, you will do the birthing thing right instead of that screaming maniac scene you starred in last time. This production will not have the frail girl who could not face the reality of a new body next to her wanting to suck from those breasts that did not know how to make milk. You are a real woman now.

Mac had not recovered from our labor room horror show, in spite of the fact that he adored Greg. No promises from me could assure him that we could have a different experience this time. He took on the role as our "decider," articulating the last-and-only word. Women friends who got the drift of this ongoing fight offered suggestions such as pin pricks in the condom stash in the bedside table. But devious I did not do. I wanted a peer relationship, conversation, joint-decision making, even if those words did not roll off my tongue at that time. I knew this so-called partnership had a fatal flaw.

Depression then came on like an eighteen-wheeler whose brakes failed on the downhill. I had managed to keep this careening darkness away many times earlier in my life, this time the insidious malady came full-force. I felt powerless and easily took on the role of a helpless victim. Mac loomed larger than life as "the man" to "my wife" in the game of creating a "happy little home." I had campaigned for him, and worked to secure his unanimous-elected position as Chairman of the Board in our marriage. I made myself into the injured party. Anger and hurt raged. I continued to turn it on myself.

"Take these," one of the base doctors commanded. I'm guessing he was peddling Valium to lots of wives living half-lives on the base. Soon I realized this medication did not solve the problem, I felt like a walking zombie and hated living a flat-lined life; I tossed the pills. Something beyond my known awareness saved me from being one of those Momma's Little Helper junkies of that era.

Those were the days when doctors, mostly men, saw it as their duty to "save" women from the difficult task of claiming their power. God forbid that we might awaken to some choices about life that went beyond those our mothers' had. Husbands made the big decisions and we kept the house clean, cooked the meals, tended the babies and did it all with tense smiles on our faces. At least that seemed to be my worldview, my lot, the role life handed me.

I learned to keep my pain hidden, to go to Wives Club meetings and play bridge with a confident and capable countenance. We talked about our husbands' jobs and squadron gossip. We shared housekeeping and child-raising tips and just kept smiling. My pain and depression were my secret. I talked to no one about it, not even my best friends. I was embarrassed and thought if only I were smarter I could figure out how to cope. The country elected JFK as President during this period. Changes were happening in the country, but not in my world. I was stuck in the mire of entrenched patriarchal traditions.

This pattern continued for me through the next seven years. The gloom followed through five years in Moses Lake, Washington and then one year in Riverside, California, the year I turned 30. The musical *Hair* became a hit on Broadway during this time. I listened to "The Age of Aquarius" and saw the naked bodies on the stage in L.A. at the Music Center. "Let the sun shine in" they shouted. They spoke to me inviting me to break out of disempowering patterns with Mac and The Wives. I knew I had to wake up and let light into my depressed soul.

We then moved to Omaha, Nebraska, and an avalanche of changes pounded us. Mac's brother Sam died soon after we settled in at Offutt Air Force Base, the home of the Strategic Air Command. We were devastated. Death had not been in our awareness and certainly not the death of a forty-three-year-old brother. Until that time, I felt as though I had an unlimited amount of days to figure out what was important, how to get out of this morass where I had been living. The thought that I could be dead and gone in a short time made me step back and take a new look at where my creative energy was being focused.

I began a serious study of alternative religions; at least they were an alternative to my "old-time religion" which, clearly, no longer worked for me. I discovered reincarnation theories, as I read about Bridey Murphy, Edgar Casey and lots of books on Eastern Philosophy. My mental floodgates opened and nothing was off limits. I sought out palm readers, did past-life regression, astrology, and had my aura read. I tried anything and everything that I could imagine. These ideas took me on a journey far from the back roads of conservative

South Georgia. Most of the people I came into contact with seemed to be suspicious of this search. Other seekers, like me, became my best friends.

Mac was too busy with his grief over the death of his brother, and with his own work, to even quiz me about the latest shifts in my quest. This longer branch that I hung out on belonged only to me. I loved the change, even with little understanding of this strange territory with its new thoughts, questions and possibilities—a new *me* started to take shape.

I felt as though I had awakened from a trance in which I, like so many married women, had lived the life of a mime, silently mimicking the motions of the "happy wife." At the age of thirty-two, I was born again. I heard no one singing, "Just as I Am", the way they do in the Baptist Church when you walk down front to make a public statement of faith. Instead of an "altar call," I felt that a bolt of lightning had hit me. None of my old friends seemed to have been struck, they mindlessly kept up the same old routines. After all, our husbands were risking their lives to keep the Communists from our doorsteps. We were safe. How about lunch? Maybe bridge or let's go shopping.

During this time, many people built bomb shelters and school children performed frequent drills, "duck and cover," to prepare them for a nuclear attack. My nightmares were more about the little prisons most of us had settled for at this cultural moment. I felt rage at the injustice that I saw and the phoniness of the life I had believed in before the trance ended. Again much of that rage, I directed right back at me.

> *Why did I wait so long to notice the obvious? Why isn't it obvious to everyone? Those scenes on the news do tell me, I'm not alone, but I'm not out there, I'm here in this house on a military base.*

Until this time, I had been more like Mama with her "ask no questions" policy. Clearly, too much questioning was not acceptable for a military wife. I ventured into uncharted territory. My husband had top-secret clearance. I did not. I always voted the way he suggested and truly believed his decisions were universally correct. Until this moment in time, there was never a doubt in my mind that my good man didn't know all the "right stuff."

Mac mostly stood back and witnessed my metamorphosis with few objections. However he did rear up like a stallion when he knew I was meeting with one of the base chaplains for some counseling. When we had one of our head-to-head confrontations, he often ended the debate with, "Chris, there is no middle ground here. We need a decision and *I have made it*. That's just the way it is." The thought of me discussing our difficulties with anyone was a major threat to the Major. He wanted to keep me on a short leash. In his world, he outranked me, and rank determined everything: "Never question an officer's commands."

Our differences surfaced with decisions about how we spent money, whether we would have another baby and whether we would live on base or choose a civilian neighborhood. Living on base always won out, we had only one child, and Mac, of course, controlled our finances. He was the commander of our home and I stayed pissed off, (an expression that really pissed him off). He hated my fierce and increasingly furious, trashy mouth.

Deep in my innermost being, I knew that I had bought into a lie up until this time. I knew now that I had power, but found it difficult to tap into it with Mac as my partner/ companion. These feelings brought rage that came in huge outbursts spewing all over anyone within three feet of me, especially Mac. I quit smoking at that time, and most likely, folks thought my bitchy ways came from nicotine withdrawal.

Maps were not available in this new territory. The instruction manual I had been given previously said: "Be nice, smile, keep your legs together, wear a girdle and don't dare jiggle." Loretta Young, icon of the 50's and 60's, showed us the way as she swished onto our TV screens in high heels, blouses with just a bit of cleavage peeking through and full skirts held out by crinoline petticoats. I had always thought that I would one day grow into a graceful woman like her. Instead, I let myself jiggle both physically and metaphorically. Good-bye Loretta—hello Janis Joplin!

Poor Mac did not recognize this foreign creature now occupying our bed. It had probably never crossed his mind that I might change and grow into something other than the genteel southern woman of his dreams. He was raised in a small town that was utterly different from my life in Savannah, where moving from Brady Street to a Housing Project was a step up for my family. "Street smart" would probably best describe me, and Mac was more the class president, the "May King" type. He had movie star good looks and the charming ways every mother dreamed of for her daughter.

"You always seem to be campaigning for the title of May King," I screamed at him in one of our many loud confrontations. "Too bad you didn't marry the damn May Queen!" For sure, he would not have cast a vote for me in the contest for "Miss Congeniality."

His comeback most often came in this query, "Chris, can't you just be civil?" He had a grandmother named Civility, so he was genetically and ideologically predisposed to the notion that a woman's role was to be civil first and always. I did not measure up to his version of a lady. I had begun to see uncivil systems operating all around me in the big world and certainly in the little space that I occupied. Mac seemed to be happy in his role as defender of global peace. He had his mission and mine appeared to be the opposite, a disturber of his peace. I could not keep secrets and I could not keep my mouth shut.

Mac held a staff position at Offutt Air Force Base and his flying time came from any opportunities available. He had no regular crew or flying schedule, though keeping his pilot status required that he get a certain amount of time each month in the cockpit. His aircraft, the KC 135, mainly refueled the B52 Bombers in mid-air—these big guys who presumably kept the Russians from our doorsteps and depended on the tankers to get them to their targets. We on Strategic Air Command bases accepted this mission as normal, ordinary life.

On one of these flight days, he came home and I asked, "Have you eaten since being away all night?" Greg and I had just finished our breakfast, and I was prepared to make Mac his favorite grits and eggs.

He said, "I had breakfast on the flight. The steward served steak and eggs."

"A steward? You're pulling my leg," I said. "Whoever heard of a steward on a 135 flight?"

He explained that this was not the ordinary refueling mission, but instead he had spent the night flying on the in-air command post.

"Why in the hell do we need a flying command post?" I asked incredulously. He carefully explained how Generals from other SAC bases came in to serve time as commander of this 24-hour, seven-days-a-week defense project.

"In the event all on the ground are wiped out," he answered plainly, as though it was the most ordinary thing, like asking, "What time is *The Andy Griffith Show* coming on today?"

This reply left me speechless. In that moment, a major explosion happened in my awareness. Until I heard this simple statement, I had no clue about the insane stuff that so many of us in America accepted as ordinary life.

My god, this is nuts—the way it is when you live life by the war plan. All these folks with eagles and stars on their shoulders, showing visible evidence of their importance, make my head hurt and my mind whirl. We might all be dead, but rest easy—there will be a command post in the air. Who will they be commanding? Suppose the replacement gets blown up in the big blast? Would the one in the air just command until they ran out of fuel and then die the hero's death? Who would there be to do the 21-gun salute and drape the coffin with a flag? No wonder I had been questioning my sanity—I'd been living in a world even crazier, and certainly more lethal, than the one in which I'd grown up.

Mac did not hear my words; I kept silent and continued to stare at him with what must have conveyed a "Say what?" look. He went on about his business, end of discussion.

I wish I could say I became a community activist at this point, honoring my impulse by taking to the streets to protest the wrongs of the world; I didn't. Instead, I trained as a crisis counselor—the so-called "crazies" became the only folks that I could relate to with any confidence. The voices of those calling to ask for help brought comfort to me—they were my people. Occasionally, I did find an exception, like the caller who grossed me out with descriptions of his sexual perversion. I listened as long as I could bear, then, as he transitioned to new graphic details, I hung up my phone. He did not call asking for help, he only wanted an audience—I had not signed up for that job.

I also disconnected from the women who had been sitting across the bridge table from me, bragging about their husbands' latest promotion or spitting disbelief regarding his being overlooked. I knew the folks on the hotline much better. We were in the same dark pit and, while I was talking with them, I began to see how I had these same feelings and self-destructive tendencies. For the first time in my life, I began to take a serious look at the patterns of my family-of-origin and to see how these issues had more control over me than I wanted to admit. And, in the process, I became my own counselor.

As the war in Vietnam raged on, so did I. My whole being started to take on a new shape. The kaleidoscope in my head kept turning images and new perspectives appeared. I found the courage to stand up and say my piece of truth. It spewed out incoherent gibberish. Greg and Mac lived in the center of my personal war zone.

******

The woman who exited from the canyon in April of 1991 through the east gate did not resemble the broken creature that had entered through the south gate on the previous day. My spirit knew this step was onto holy ground. I could only manage to follow my hunch by keeping the van pointing in the right direction while waves of new awareness rolled over me. I saw the world through a new lens. The Four Corners area where Arizona, New Mexico, Utah and Colorado meet had an "other-worldly" feel to it that matched my inner consciousness. My "four corners" were coming together on that same spot. From my motel in Kayenta that night, I watched the sunset while I lay naked on my bed allowing my pores to sponge up the last drops of the day.

I moseyed along for two days and let myself just wallow in the bare vastness of the native land. My van became my own roving monastery, as I drove past icons that dotted the landscape. By the time I arrived in New Mexico, for my second time, the pulse of the planet had become a loud drumbeat. I stood on the edge of the Rio Grande Gorge on a dirt road, played gospel music and danced. I can still see that spot in the Carson National Forest where the realization came that my life had reached the place where I felt in my bones that this was as good as it would ever get and, no matter what the future held, I would be okay. I had been awakened. Like a cosmic orgasm, I had a feeling of union with **life**.

This experience is difficult to describe. C.S. Lewis's book, *Surprised by Joy*, recounts three different times in his childhood when he had an out-of-the-ordinary awareness, "a moment of joy," he called it. He goes on to tell his readers that if they have not had similar moments in their lives, they might as well read no further; they will not understand. My two-month period on the road was such a time. Possibly only those who have also felt the urge to search for answers that lack specific questions will have any clue as to what my words mean.

Old thought patterns seemed to have been erased. My brain waves had a new cadence. Except for impersonal communication with motel desk clerks or food service people, I had little contact with living persons. My daily telephone conversation with Mac barely counted. His monosyllabic responses did little to help me feel anchored to another human being. Northern New Mexico was new territory, just like the uncharted territory in my head. New thoughts came from all directions—truly a desert experience.

In retrospect, it seemed to me that the spirits of native cultures became my guides rather than the "desert fathers" within my own tradition. I had almost no knowledge of those who had lived on this continent before white people came and took over. Fascinated by these cultures whose ways were more in sync with nature, I fell in love with their art as well as their wisdom. I had *deja vu* experiences everyday. I know something in my DNA remembered a past life in the pueblo.

When the ranger at one of my stops talked about the rules that governed life in the native community, I could barely keep my emotion from showing. He said, "The rooms in the pueblo and the garden land belonged to the women. When divorce happened, which it did, the man would just move out." This was tribal law. This tribal law made sense to me and certainly would have settled lots of those control issues that messed up my own volatile marriage. However, I knew I was the one who had to leave our home and that my leave-taking would only last two months. I had no plan to claim our Quincy home as mine alone and I never doubted my desire to share my living space with Mac.

Again, I found my way back to Tepayac and spent time with residents of The Center for Contemplation and Action. I could see patterns of their lifestyle that I had missed the first time around, simple things like gardening, composting, and attention to habits of wasteful consumption. Water is precious in the desert, as it should be everywhere, but at Tepayac, we learned new ways to conserve everything: flush only when necessary, short showers, compost the vegetable scraps, etc. Up until then, spiritual discipline only meant something like Bible reading, confessing sins and praying for forgiveness—

now flushing, composting and recycling went on the list as a way to embody a lifestyle of gratitude for "our daily bread."

The world of retail had done little to prepare me for a close look directly at the spiritual pilgrims' way of life. The whole idea of women's fashion relied on changing so that last year's wardrobe could be discarded. To recycle meant you would take your old stuff to Goodwill (and be sure to get a receipt so you can take a tax deduction). I could see why the world that I had lived in for over 20 years was driving me faster than I could keep up, yet I lacked the capacity to take in all these new, slower, more mindful ways of being. Much of this new way of seeing had to be filed away where I could later retrieve it in tiny bits and pieces.

In order to see what was before me, I had to slow down. These spiritual lessons could not come through unless I took my foot off the pedal and gave up the manic pace. Quiet and stillness had never been my goal. I was about doing, accomplishing, achieving success—all those characteristics I so disliked in Mac. The hard part came in integrating contemplative consciousness during ordinary life, not just while on a two-month pilgrimage. I knew better than to set myself up for failure by stretching beyond my reach. Each day, I awoke to doubts about my ability to commit to these big changes. Could I possibly take the new habits—the new *me*— into my old world? Would I put new wine in old wineskins? Who would I be when I got back home? Would I be seduced by the pull of the frantic world to conform in order to fit in? I understood why some folks chose a monastic life. It can be hard to live counter-culturally with all the pressures, noise and temptations of life in the "real world."

After New Mexico, I made arrangements to visit with old friends who lived in Arkansas. Jo and Thurston had been our neighbors in Moses Lake. He retired from the Air Force, studied law, and became a county judge. Jo, ("Luna Jo" to loved ones), was a high school guidance counselor. They, like me, came from a lower-middle class, Georgia background. But unlike me, they went to work getting the education they had missed. I admired them and their free-thinking ways. Thurston was absolutely the most aware person in the area of social justice that I had ever met. He claimed to be an atheist. I delighted in telling him that he was the most Christian atheist I had ever known.

The idea of ending this enlivening two-month saga with the two of them felt just right. They lived in a big old house in Rogers, Arkansas. When I arrived, the door had a note on it telling me to come on in; they would soon be home. I walked in to the welcoming scent of bread baking in a bread machine.

We had common memories of life when their three kids and Greg had run in and out of our side-by-side houses. We had so much shared history and spoke the same South-Georgia lingo. They grew up on the Savannah River in Augusta and I was downriver from them.

I told them about the events leading up to my decision to strike out on my own. They could understand my pain around war. Like me, with greater exposure to "the real world," they had changed their points of view since our days long ago on SAC bases during the Cold War.

I had a story to tell and the part that the Panama Invasion played in my awakening could not be told to just anyone. I knew Jo and Thurston could hear my truth and empathize. I seized the moment and unloaded the pain that I had carried alone for over the past year.

"Last year, Greg received the Mackay Trophy," I said. Thurston's eyes lit up. He knew the meaning of those words.

The trophy is given to the pilot and the crew for the most meritorious flight of the year.

"You know Greg's work is in Special Operations, his airplane is the 130 Gunship." Thurston again nodded knowingly.

"He commanded the mission that destroyed the headquarters of Manuel Noriega." I did not have to tell them about the fact that this dictator our country was hell bent on capturing and bringing to trial also happened to be a distinguished graduate of our infamous School of the Americas in Columbus, Georgia. The U.S. had arrogantly set him up, and then called the troops in with the big guns in order to rectify the screw-up.

I ended my monologue by describing the scene when I flew with Mac to Washington to attend the award ceremony at the Pentagon. On the flight to Washington, it must have appeared to other passengers nearby that Mac and I were having some domestic crisis—my tears flowed without ceasing.

A good night's sleep in the DC Hilton helped me to pull myself together. The next day we all assembled in the five-sided vault of a building. I worked hard to stay focused and to look the part of the proud mother. To say I was conflicted would be an understatement. I have no words to describe the rift I felt in my soul. There was no doubt that I was bigheaded about the accomplishment of my child. After all, this was a big deal, but couldn't we find a big deal without weapons that kill people?

When asked if I considered myself to be a pacifist, I'd say, "I would be one, but I am not active enough to claim that moniker. Those folks are more evolved and involved than I am." The most difficult test that I faced was "turning the other cheek" to those who accused me of disloyalty to my son simply because I did not wave the flag and shout a patriotic "hurrah!" every time the U.S. marched into another war that brought about more bloodshed. Without a doubt, Greg and I continued to like, and yes love, one another. The very idea that my beliefs about war would ever cause me to disconnect from my offspring was, and always will be, absurd. That kind of reasoning was part of what sent me running from the Deep South, where I often felt strangled by hateful, narrow points of view that fell out of the mouths of the small-minded.

"If you see me protesting at the gate to the base when you drive in to go to work, wave to me," I told Greg. Most likely, he would yell, "Go home, Mama!" We could then have a friendly glass of wine together that evening and neither of us would question the motives of the other.

Conversation with Jo and Thurston gave me the closure I needed to make the return to Mac and our home in Quincy. I told Mac that I was staying one day longer than I had planned. I wanted to surprise him by coming in a day earlier than he expected.

In and Out of Business

EVERYTHING THAT IRRITATES US ABOUT OTHERS CAN LEAD US TO AN UNDERSTANDING OF OURSELVES.

CARL JUNG

IN 1970, MAC, AT THE age of forty-two, made the decision to retire from the military and I, at age thirty-three, connected with a vague yearning from a childhood fantasy and decided to buy a retail shop from Mac's niece. Suzie had owned *Suzie's Wigs etc.* for two years and had a bit of a spotty history, leaving the balance sheet a mess. I jumped in simply because it felt right—god knows why. The wig business had boomed in the 60's, and Suzie vaulted into the middle of it and muddled her way through until, with no thought of the consequences, I dove in. "I have always wanted to be in business; let me have it!" I pronounced. My feeble rationale was, "If I do not do this at this moment, I will spend the rest of my life wondering about what could have been."

The line from Paul Simon's song "Slip Sliding Away" best describes my belief—"a bad day is when I lie in bed and think of things that might have been." That line could go on my tombstone. It has caused me to do lots of foolish things or, as some might say, to look like a total fool.

There is no doubt, I must have looked out of place on College Avenue in Tallahassee, my shop was right next door to The Head Shop and I came straight out of the Officer's Wives Club on Offutt Air Force Base. I watched the barefooted, unwashed young folks darting in and out of the shop next door to buy their drug paraphernalia. I must have been there for at least two months before I realized what a "head shop" sold. "*Head of what?*" I wondered.

I decided to drop "Suzie's" and "wigs" from the name so it then became merely "etc." The wigs did stay in the inventory and, for the first year, I acted as though false hair was an item that I understood. The flips, shags and afros were displayed right next to the small inventory of women's apparel and accessories. I became an instant authority on stuff that to this day I know zip about.

Selling comes naturally to me, I've always thought that I could, if need be, sell used cars. Afro wigs required no special skill to sell, they were our bestsellers. My experience as a customer of women's fashion did nothing to prepare me for the position I took on the other side of the counter. Customers must think the person who asks, "May I help you?" actually knows something about the product they are looking to find. I did not know squat about the apparel trade and less than squat about wigs. Ignorance of the product did not stop me from spending my days responding in some affirming way to every woman who walked through the door of *etc.*

I had no business plan. Each day I started with a blank script and filled in the squares as each new need arose. I could do alterations if necessary and opinions about fashion rolled off the tip of my tongue. Some days the sales came to zero and my way of coping then became a headstand in the stock room.

Prior to Mac's retirement, I had started a yoga practice. This upside down position out of the view of customers helped me to recharge my battery and keep a positive outlook. This practice must have worked, since at the end of my first year, the CPA told me that I had made a profit.

"Where is this profit?" I naively asked. "It is in your inventory," he said.

Damn, why not in my pocket?

I had paid myself no salary and I had no employees. Mac told me that all I was doing was burning up a car transporting myself the twenty miles each day from Quincy to Tallahassee. I bluffed and said, "You'll see." I no more believed this venture would work than he did. Arrogance and false pride kept me showing up and opening the doors everyday. My goal in the beginning was to get to the break-even place and then quietly fold my tent and steal away.

I thought maybe then that I could find a life of contentment in Quincy, i.e., playing bridge and responding to the favorite subjects of many of the local women—whether the maid showed up this morning and, if not, how one might cope with this awful domestic crisis. When such thoughts crossed my mind, I would have to bring myself back to reality and remember that I had given up bridge three years before and I never had a maid.

When the breakeven point came, I was hooked on this new image of myself as a successful woman in the garment trade. I loved advertising, buying, getting to know customers, almost everything about running a store. And, much to my surprise, Mac began to take the venture more seriously.

After five years, my little shop became a bustling downtown business in Tallahassee three blocks from the campus of Florida State University, just around the corner from the State Capitol. Who would ever have imagined such a thing would happen?

Mac came on board as a partner and we opened a second store in Quincy, right on the courthouse square, catty-cornered across from McMillan's Barber Shop, where Mac could keep an eye on his aging Dad who not only did the barber thing, but also was the repository for all the local news. Mac became our office manager and I continued to handle the creative part. Greg, in high school by this time, helped out, too. This mom, pop and son operation became the main focus of our family.

One day, while remodeling our Tallahassee store, I accidentally did a back flip off a ladder and landed head first on the stock room concrete floor. I went in and out of consciousness while being rushed to the ER with sirens blaring. I came to consciousness with Mac and Greg standing by the bedside. They told me I had a few stitches in my head. I later learned that Mac thought for sure I was dead as he knelt over me in the stockroom. He had done some mouth-to-mouth while waiting for the medics. Mac helped me off the table and told me I looked like the walking wounded back from fighting the Yankees.

The doctor said, "You will have to keep an eye on her for a few days, she will be confused and irritable." Without missing a beat, Mac asked, "How will I know when it is over?" Greg loves to tell this story and I am sure that there were some days that Mac thought I had not come to the end of my confusion and irritability.

Greg's voice could be heard on our radio and TV spots singing our store's jingle. *"You've got a lot to say about the way you look today—etc., general store for the woman of today."* What a team the three of us had become, so different from that raging woman who kept the household in a swivet back in Omaha.

Greg's favorite way of introducing himself when he went off to college in Tennessee was to say, "I grew up in women's clothes." The truth of the matter is the whole family grew in myriad ways during those years. For all of us, our bond went beyond imagination.

My fights about money with Mac ended when I started to make deposits into the family coffers. I had leverage like never before. Now we could stand eye-to-eye, toe-to- toe. Finally, my voice had power and I did not even have to turn up the volume. I cannot claim any credit for finding my way to this new position. The gift merely fell into my lap.

The part of my work that did not come easily was the part that had to do with employees. I quickly found that I had many of the same characteristics I found so ugly in Mac. I liked being in control and had no patience with anyone who did not do things exactly the way I thought they should be done. Two minutes late to work and my unmerciful bitch came out. Most of our employees were college students and some of the more fragile ones could not stand up under my scrutiny. I have sent many freshman sorority girls home to be comforted by their mamas as I did not take them on to raise as my own. Others flourished in the fast-paced, constantly changing world of fashion, and we made a great team.

The third store opened soon after the second one—this one on the north side of Tallahassee, the moneyed side of town. After ten years, our downtown store closed and we replaced it with a mall store, something I said I would never do. By that time, I knew enough to swallow my pride, eat my words, change my mind and go in the direction of the customer. Downtown business became a thing of the past and malls kidnapped our former customers.

Working with Mac added new passion to our life. Fighting over business decisions kept us sparring; it became the glue that was previously missing in our relationship. I was the visionary and he was the dependable, Republican, fiscal conservative, the numbers and "just-the-facts" person. We knew we needed the other, but oh, how the sparks would fly!

Mac had his office in our Quincy store where we also had the stock room. I only worked in the Tallahassee stores where the customers were mostly women whom I could easily understand. The Quincy customer might ask questions that I could not answer, like "Has anyone in my group bought this outfit?" First of all, I did not know which "group" was hers. The sales people in Quincy were "in the know." They not only knew who belonged in which group, they also kept records of purchases, so they could check to make sure they were giving the right answer.

My all-time favorite recollection was the woman who came in one day, saw a rack of coordinates we had just received, and said, "Now don't sell that outfit to anyone in my group. I did not know you would be getting it in and I bought it in Jacksonville last week." She holds the record in my file cabinet of privileged people. She is the same person who said to me one day that she did not like shopping in a mall. I agreed with her and thought: *At last I have found a common bond.* She went on to state her reason, "My arms get too tired from carrying all those packages around."

"I know what you mean," I said, silently grimacing.

Another popular query was, "Do you know what folks will be wearing to "so-and-so's" party?" I had no clue about "so and so" even giving a party. Occasionally, I would overhear women asking, "Did you make the cut for the big party?" "Making the cut" seemed to be a high priority. That statement forever reminded me of my days at Savannah High. I felt sad for those who could not "make the cut" and, at the same time, grateful that I had no desire to be on such a list. Still, our sales were dependent on many of those big parties, and it would have been stupid to ignore that fact. When it came to making money, I knew when to go silent; my potentially-alienating opinions and preferences were seldom voiced.

A friend told me that she could always tell when she walked into my store if I was having a good day. She said my eyes brightened each time the cash register made the little ka-ching sound. I did love tracking sales and seeing the graph climbing each year. Shameless in my quest for profit making, I offered no apologies for my mercenary ways.

On the subject of making money, Mac and I stayed in sync. We went to the Apparel Market together, the site of our major battles. He trusted my judgment on style, but when it came to the dollar figure he still thought he had the last word and sometimes the only word. The Atlanta Merchandise Mart was built around an atrium and many times I would look down from the third or fourth floor and picture shoving Mac over the edge! He was relentless, and I felt suffocated by his need to control me. His lecture on over-buying started at 9:00 a.m., the moment we'd walk through the revolving door. By lunchtime my murderous thoughts had a total grip on me. In the evening, we would go out and have a great meal in the big city and finally, my body would relax. The next day the process would repeat. The dance was familiar and somehow both of us seemed to believe this was the only way we could get the job done.

When we built a new house, Greg, age seventen, suggested we build a soundproof office. He was sick of listening to our "decision-making" process with its usual progression from loud to louder. Mac's desire to make money and be successful in business softened some of his control issues with me. For the first time in our marriage, I was doing something financially empowering and I loved the new image, and could use this new power in ways I had only been able to imagine before. Finally, I had some *big guns*; the good military man understood this kind of deal. We both thrived on our new battlefield.

Customers and employees numbered among my best friends. The money came in with each new store, giving me greater and greater confidence. We raised our son, managed to do the parent thing well, traveled together to Europe and had interesting folks coming and going in and out of our home. Friends and family sang around the player piano as I pumped out rousing old tunes. My strong legs were my musical talent. Greg and Mac had the vocal gift. Life was fun and full. Through my eyes, it looked like the all-American success story—we must have appeared to be the Norman Rockwell poster family of the 70's and 80's.

Our family was active in a Methodist Church that was within walking distance from our house. My theology was not exactly in the mainstream, but this paradox was not a problem for me. Mac had grown up in this Church and Greg had been baptized there when we'd returned from Turkey. Often, in Sunday school, someone would say, "Let's hear the flaming liberal point of view," as everyone turned in my direction—I didn't hold back. In a left-handed sort of way, I felt valued. I had no doubt that the minority party needed to be heard and I was happy to carry that progressive banner with pride.

In 1981, about the time Greg finished college and my dad finally died after holding the family hostage for years with raging dementia, I started to ask some new, even bolder, questions. I began looking in a different direction and could not quite identify the felt need. I experienced an intense longing that had always been with me but, this time, I had no idea what would fill it. A therapist helped to prop me up and, for a time, it seemed as though I would manage to stay on the old track and get my body moving each day. However, there was a noticeable change: after eleven years the retail business began to lose its first-place priority in my world. Volunteer work filled more spaces on the calendar. I made new friends. The search continued for several more years while a vague discontent hovered over me, especially in my dreams.

A recurring nightmare was one where Mac was ignoring me and, in a very cruel way, taunting me. I would wake sobbing, yet had no skills to discuss these night terrors with him. I knew enough to realize that dreams may not actually be about the person in them, but they could represent an aspect of my own psyche.

> *Who in me is taunting me and refusing to communicate? God, how complex! Why can't I just be normal and content with life as it is? Why do I always want something more? Self-centered bitch!*

After tewnty-one years, my drive to stay in business utterly disappeared. The world was spinning faster than I could follow and the voices screaming in my head could no longer be ignored. I had the same clarity about getting out that I had about getting in. We had four stores, yet I could not find it in my soul to care in the least what the trends were for the coming season. I agonized over abandoning employees and Mac, but also knew that if I stayed, I would help no one and my spirit would wither and die.

The fourth store had been open for only one year. Mac, who seemed quite sullen at the time, wanted this expansion and I capitulated hoping that this new project would cheer him up. I had been urging him to see a doctor to get a check-up. His bent-over walk and lack of expression looked like the anvil of depression. I would make appointments for him but he would cancel them just before the appointed day. He was slippery and I was out of my league in dealing with this problem. A new store was my solution, my best idea.

The new little cottage shop catered to the older women of the town, unlike our other store on the courthouse square. I was fifty-three and, at the time, thought I could find the right styles to suit this clientele; since I saw myself fast approaching their age and stage. What was ironic is that I hated those waistless *chemises* done in the no-iron print fabrics. "Get your judgments out of the way and just write the orders," the merchandise-manager voice in me commanded.

The solution backfired: the store brought out the crazies in me. Everyday, I found myself in fits of rage, hating everything about this "cute little shop" that we named Gregory's. Worst of all, Mac still looked the same, with little life and certainly no spark of creativity for this or any new venture. This "medicine" of mine had no transformative effect.

When I tried to explain my feelings, he would respond with one of his famous "you statements." He would say, "Chris, your problem is …" I would then use every word he detested in my vocabulary, the discourse that I had learned from Daddy. I would tell him that I did not need his remedy for what *he* thought was *my* problem. "Could you possibly take another look and just *maybe* consider that you have a problem, too?" Truly he thought that he could fix me, and fixing himself seemed to never enter his mind. These scenes could not keep playing on the "happy family" network—it was ugly, really crass, and I imagine some of the neighbors were bearing witness.

When I could no longer keep up the sparring, I made the "get out of town" plan. First order of business included closing two stores. Then, I packed my van with books, mostly novels that would distract me, my journals to then bring focus and, of course, jeans, sweat shirts and hiking boots. I was determined to head west.

"There is a feeling of death all around me here in Quincy," I moaned as Mac gave me a blank stare. "Run for your life!" an unknown voice screamed.

The Return

MY CHECK-IN AT A MOTEL in Mississippi was the usual: view of the sunset, room next to the office, and bedspread in the corner. But this one would be the last. Tomorrow, I would be back in my house where my soothing Jacuzzi tub awaited me and lord knows what else—for sure I had no guess, possibly a lynch mob on the front lawn.

Insecurities about my ability to return to my home and to my husband, with any measure of grace, paralyzed me. My worst fear was that I would let myself cave into fits of rage and anger. The paradoxical image of the contemplative, foul-mouthed, dish-throwing maniac and total fool was the cartoon illustration that I drew in my head.

> *God, what a joke I am. Can I return to the role of wife, keeper of house and garden? Will I be pulled back into that store just two blocks away from home?*

Am I any better equipped to deal with Mac and his impenetrable ways?

How will I silence that scathing voice that's been passed down through my genes that continues to have me judging who's right and whose people are better or worse? Can I let go of all my destructive habits or is it too late? Am I set in concrete or am I flexible enough to be reshaped? I know something in me has shifted—I'm changed, but who will I be in that not-me setting?

The questions won out, all my answers scored zero. The surprise tactic worked on Mac. He looked shocked when he found me walking in the back door with my van now parked in its familiar spot in our garage.

She's back! The locks have not been changed, keep looking for any positive signs, just act like you have been out shopping and stayed longer than you realized.

We started a hot topic the moment after the welcome home kiss and hug. He returned reflexively to his stubborn habit of telling me what I should feel. Just as predictably, I returned to my habit of telling him that he was full of shit. This familiar dance started immediately. Mac seemed extremely touchy; an innocent remark about the oppressive heat that morning in Mississippi set him off. In his usual correcting voice, he said, "Chris, this is not oppressive." I replied, "You start telling me what I am supposed to feel and I will get right back in that van and leave again."

Jesus Christ, I'm home—this is so familiar. What a joke! I can't even hold it together for the first hour back in the real world. What a phony.

That condemning voice came at me with a hatchet. The fight continued while we drove to a Tallahassee restaurant as well as at the table while eating dinner. Back in our bedroom, still no cease-fire declared. Then, I must have finally looked into Mac's eyes and had a glimpse of his wounded manhood.

Pick your battles, Chris. This one is stupid. You are in your own home and looking right at the man you've freely chosen to share it with—suck it up.

I adjusted my attitude, gave up defending myself and, all of a sudden, there was my lover in the room. I had missed him and wanted him back in my bed. At that point, we moved into familiar territory, the place where we were equals. We both relaxed; the fight was over.

The real test was life in Quincy and the pull of that store just around the corner where I had invested so much of myself. We still had one in Tallahassee but that was far enough away that the magnetic tug could not be felt. I was one strange creature—no longer a businesswoman and feeling like a poor excuse for a wife. What was I? I had been reborn for sure, but I felt a stranger to myself. I felt ill at ease both in my home and in my body.

Family and friends did not flock to the house to welcome me home. Certainly, no one had any interest in hearing about my "dark night of the soul." It seemed that I now spoke a foreign language and that most conversations after my return went on in my head. Mac would occasionally leave the store and come home to check on me. I must have looked like a nervous rabbit caught in the headlights, unable to figure out whether to go forward or run back to my comfortable hole. Mac then took on a pained look, leaving me as he found me so he could return to his comfort-zone hole—the office where most of the day he would sit at a desk and punch numbers into a calculator.

About the only relief I could find was to sit in my Jacuzzi, the spot that was previously home to my antique claw foot, "right-out-in-the-open" tub. Classical music played in the background and a glass of wine rested on the edge as I went into places in my soul that were wholly unfamiliar. I called it my daily baptism.

I shed buckets of tears in this ritual, as over and over I grieved the years "living" within the tight shell of a person who had been masquerading as me. She was not a bad person. I couldn't kill her; I had to love her. Later, I saw how well she had served me before this time. Now, I could manage without her armor of protection. Still, I felt embarrassed to see how shallow and mean-spirited she could be when threatened. What an illusion I had created about being a charitable, loving person. Underneath that façade lived a woman who was capable of unspeakable acts of unkindness. My harsh judgments about others had turned me into exactly the same thing I so rejected in them.

That long-ago awakening experienced in Omaha had only spotlighted the outer world and opened my eyes to heretofore unnoticed lack of social justice. The bathtub moments washed the hard, outer layer away and cut to the quick where my blind side became illuminated. I had not seen how I had always looked to the outer world to give me a feeling of self-worth. I had been blind to my narrow, critical ways of judging others. The biggest point that I had missed was this aggressive voice in my head loudly telling me how wrong everyone was for not being more loving and accepting. That voice slashed away at me all the time; here I thought it was only summing up the inadequacy of everyone else.

Those daily "baptism" rituals did not leave me clean and totally pure, but they sure did take away some of the steel coating that had previously protected me. I would tell Mac at times, "I feel as though I have been sanded down." Every nerve was raw and right on the surface. He would listen respectfully, but it was obvious that he had no clue about the meaning of my words. I needed to say it though and, at that time, he happened to be the designated listener—the only body in sight.

The preacher from our Methodist Church finally came to call on me about one month after my return. He said, "I did not come sooner because I had to get over my anger toward you. I was told that you would never return to church as long as I was there." I told him that I had never said or thought such a thing. My leaving the church had nothing to do with him; it was only about me.

I guess he spoke for lots of folks on that day. They believed my behavior said something about them. This explained their rote responses like, "Glad to see you!" when we had eye-to-eye encounters. I never gave my preferred reply: "Bullshit!" Of course they were not glad to see me. I was too strange for them to look at directly. If they *saw* me, really looked me in the eye, they may catch my strange malady— god forbid, odd notions might creep in. This disorder could be contagious. Running away from home and spending time in convents, leaving the traditional church, this was not the way *normal* people live or, at least, not these people.

Without hesitation, I can say that those two months away from Quincy were the most important and even happiest 60 days of my whole life. I felt the most *me*—the most free— and yet so aware of my flaws and weaknesses. My neurotic dependence on the "god in the sky," like Santa Claus, died a slow death, bit by tiny bit. In its place I allowed little truths to take over and feed my starved consciousness. God is no longer locked in by solid walls, the concept fits nicely in a filmy veiled place that allows fresh breezes to blow through.

The need to be validated by anyone else also lost its solid image and just drifts by from time to time. I feel certain that my earlier instincts never totally died, they only diminished amidst traditional mandates for women of my era (or *error*). Like most of the women I've known, I had expected to find the man of my dreams, hoping feelings of togetherness would take us into the joy that awaited both of us into our golden years. Those were not the words I would have used in my 30's and 40's, but by the time I hit my 50's, I saw how I had lived as though any moment the sky would open and Mac would "see the light" of true intimacy and begin to share his inner-most thoughts with me. There would be a Hallelujah chorus in the background and we would fade off into the sunset, make mad love, and then live as one complete entity into eternity.

God, how embarrassing it was to admit to myself that I had clung to this pitiful vision for as long as I could remember. Yes, I lived spring-loaded for a breakthrough that was never to come. Those of us who grew up in the days of the Prince Charming Fairy Tales were pre-wired to buy into such destructive notions. The image was subtle and had power over us, even when our mouths said something different. In no way did this successful, capable businesswoman appear to be in need of a man to make her whole. Mac certainly was not of the generation who could speak words about emotional needs. He was dedicated to making money, being competent and, most of all, being in control.

Then, some other creature moved into Mac's body; this one looked feeble and had a blank stare. The Hallelujah chorus sang off key and the picture fractured. My coping mechanism told me to pack my hiking boots and get to work finding the "me" who could navigate without a man to show me the way. Nobody would have believed what the messages in my head were saying before I stepped out on my own, before I drew my line in the sand.

One year after my return to Quincy, we moved to Tallahassee where I had friends who were more in sync with my kind of "insanity." Mac had always told me I could choose the next move, since he had been the one leading us on all the others. I cashed in this chit and we settled in an upscale townhouse near the Capitol and the University.

Mac finally had to admit that he could no longer keep up the pace of our retail business. He had held on longer than I had expected, but watching his forceful spirit continue to slip away became more painful every day. The popular belief was that he was suffering ill health due to the fact that he lived with an unstable person. Although I was never confronted directly with these accusations, a few well-meaning "friends" felt it their duty to "enlighten" me about the word on the street. I did not make an attempt to defend myself, since I was still unclear about what was going on with Mac. I only knew it was painful to witness.

We managed to sell the corporation and took off on a trip west, this time together. We had a leisurely drive, visited old friends and saw magnificent scenery.

Maybe this will do the trick. He is out from under the pressure of business and traveling together is what we do best—could enliven both of us—at least, it works for me.

It was not the golden key, but we did have some measure of joy. Some nights, we camped in the back of our van, other times we stayed in luxury rooms—our ideal mix in a vacation. Some meals were gourmet and others cheese and crackers, eaten while watching the sunset from our folding chairs. Although Mac's body and mind were losing their flexibility, his style of living remained eclectic. We thrived in the freedom of the open space of the west, and the vastness of the landscape fed our minds as we took it all in. Neither of us had ever had rigid requirements for personal comforts. For me, a bottle of wine would come high on my list and for Mac, Snickers bars. Generally, we always carried a stash of both.

In spite of wishful thinking, good judgment told me that Mac could not be restored to the healthy, upright, bright spirit, charming lover that he had been for the 65 previous years of his life. I did not feel the same despair that I had when I first set out on my pilgrimage, just the awareness that I could not hold back the increasing dimness that I saw. No matter how many breathtaking sights we witnessed, no matter how many starry nights we enjoyed, or glorious sunrises, this hovering ghost did not stop haunting us both.

There were no hiding places. We were together and yet both stuck in very solitary places. The mission I had set out on two years before had been only about me. Now I found my self in a "we" place. I had to pull up that Canyon image of light, dark, paradox, living in the abyss and just settle for not knowing.

> *Is this what I signed up for on that day in Paris when I said "oui" every time the mayor looked my way? Not being able to see the future is a blessing, but dammit, I would love to know what is coming next.*

A Hateful Answer

LIFE DOES NOT ACCOMMODATE YOU; IT SHATTERS YOU.
EVERY SEED DESTROYS ITS CONTAINER, OR ELSE THERE
WOULD BE NO FRUITION.

FLORIDA SCOTT-MAXWELL

ALMOST AS SOON AS WE returned to Tallahassee, we found ourselves in the emergency room of the hospital to deal with Mac's excruciating stomach pain. After a couple of days of testing and probing, "a strangulated stomach" was diagnosed. The mandatory surgery seemed to exacerbate his old-man look. I felt as though I was sleeping with my Daddy when we returned home. He shuffled about in a frail and pitiful manner. The thought that we could end in this kind of predicament had frequently crossed my mind with a frightening obsessiveness.

Holy shit—I'm not ready! How did we come to this—it just snuck up and caught us off guard. I had "other" plans.

Complications from the surgery arose and the next thing I knew, we were back in the hospital for his second surgery. Greg was out of the country in another damn war,

Bosnia this time! There were calls daily, but I was on my own and emotionally overwhelmed. My usual crisis mode was to look competent and resist letting on that I needed anyone to hold me up. I just put on my "I can handle this" face.

The only difficulty I let myself acknowledge was the search for my car in the parking deck each evening as I exited the hospital. The frustration often brought me to fits of hysterical sobs.

When the surgeon came out to tell me the outcome of this second surgery, his look told me he was baffled regarding what was going on with Mac's body. We talked about the routine things—he explained to me how he had to redo the previous repairs to the stomach, because Mac had an allergic reaction to some of the artificial material that had been used in the first repair.

This all made sense, but did not address the bigger issue—why had Mac turned into this frail old man before my eyes? My brain disconnected from my voice as I said, "Charlie, when this is over, I want him checked for Parkinson's." He looked at me and said, "That might explain things." I did not tell him that I knew no one with that disease and had no idea what the symptoms were except that it made you tremble. Mac did not have that noticeable tremor, so why in this world was I saying Parkinson's?

Who is this using my voice? Where did those words come from?

Bingo! Mystery solved. I had literally found a new discerning voice. Once the problem had a name, the asking of questions became easy. Medicine could control the symptoms for a while. Even though the disease was progressive, there was time. We worked with the doctor and some expression came back to his face and a little of the old spark.

Soon after the diagnosis, I was out walking with my friend Caroline lamenting the fact that the damn disease now had control of our lives. She said, "What would you be doing if Parkinson's was not in the picture?"

"I would be planning a trip to France."

"Are you sure that is not possible?" she questioned.

On the next visit to the neurologist, I asked if Mac was up to going out of the country for an extended time. He responded, "There is no reason to believe he can't."

France, here we come. We got rail passes and took off with no hotels booked in advance. This was our favorite way to travel—no itinerary—just go and see where the spirit leads.

I wanted to spend time in the Burgundy region with The Taize Community. I had been listening to their music and knew they took in pilgrims and had daily services, mostly singing and silence and some teaching by the brothers each day.

Okay, here I go on another pilgrimage but this time, with Mac. He loved the music and the many languages in the singing. This was his kind of retreat—my linguist with his wonderful bass voice.

We rented an apartment in the Taize Village and lived the simple life of the locals. Three times each day, the bells rang out and called all to find their place on the floor or one of the low benches to enter into the life of prayer with the multi-cultural brothers who lived in the monastery.

Life was not yet over for us. Parkinson's was with us, but we managed. Mac loved the challenge of speaking French with everyone he encountered. I had my lover back, and here we were in France where we started out thirty-seven years earlier.

Caroline's question had been just the push I needed to listen to my instincts, once again. To some who knew us, it appeared as though the diagnosis was wrong. To them, we were still the adventurous, world travelers who could take off for a summer in France. We did not tell them about the many ways the disease presented itself beyond what they could see on the surface. We liked that image and did nothing to alter their view.

Mac was not helpless and he hated any conversation about being taken down by this malady. After France, I gave myself permission to even do some traveling on my own. My friend Margaret and I went to Greece and Turkey for a couple of weeks. This time I did not have the aversion to the odor of Turkish food. I delighted in returning to this exotic place and calling Mac in Tallahassee to tell him that little had changed in Istanbul since departing from there in 1959 with our seven-month old baby boy.

For our 40th anniversary, Mac and I went to Cornwall and then took the fast train through the Chunnel to France. For us, traveling and seeing the world gave us great evidence that we were alive. This we knew how to do. Talking about disease and complaining about old age was not in our lexicon. Early in our marriage, we had made a pact to live as fully for as long as we could.

We traveled, and even camped, with the grandchildren. Charlie, three years younger than Elizabeth, delighted us on a train trip to D.C. Mac loved to tell the story of four-year-old Charlie telling the taxi driver to "take us to the dinosaurs!" We became a team again and now with the fun of grand-parenting added to the mix. Life looked *almost* perfect; medicine held back the disease and we were on the move.

"Held back the disease" is not entirely accurate. Yes, we could travel and we could look somewhat normal, but that hateful disorder was always lingering. Watching Mac begin to droop, as the effects of the Sinemet wore off, was like watching a clock battery wind down. These episodes often happened in restaurants where he would slump over and take on the look of a passed-out wino. No amount of prodding could get him going until another of those little pills reprogrammed his brain. We learned to plan life around these daily interruptions. We also learned much about our power to control it and how little influence we actually had.

Many times I had to stop a stranger and ask for help to get Mac to the car or into our hotel room. Often the look told me that they thought he was drunk. I would say, "He has a neurological problem and sometimes the meds just stop working." He was a good sport, but would refuse wheelchairs where they were available and necessary. Only when he could no longer keep going, would he allow himself to be pushed in one.

A trip to upstate New York was our last one. Wheelchairs and asking a stranger for help happened more often; I knew this would be the last of our excursions. He was having bizarre side effects from meds and had recently been tested at the Parkinson's center in Tallahassee. The results told me that there had been "significant and irreparable loss of cognitive competence." I knew this, of course; having it confirmed helped and yet accepting the reality was more painful than I could bear. Long talks with myself were necessary and occasionally I allowed the "poor me" conversation with an empathic friend.

I had always depended on Mac for information. On the day I realized he could no longer read a map, I felt like screaming: "Of course, you know how to find directions, Mac! Don't act crazy!" It was beyond my comprehension that he could not look at the page and point to the spot where we wanted to go. In times such as these, my ability to swear came in handy. That was the only way I could find to express my outrage at this unreasonable turn of events. Mac not only knew the globe, he knew about the cosmos. How could he not know where the hell he was at any moment? Mac used to know how to navigate by the stars; now he seemed completely lost.

Where has my man gone?

I did not give up without a fight. I could not comprehend, nor accept, that right before my eyes, this man was devolving—the very same lover who had taught me so much about the larger world. All those platitudes I had heard about "letting go" would drift through my mind and I would feel rage: "Who is this man? He's not my husband!"

Let go? Hell, this is beyond reason.

Try as I might, like Humpty Dumpty after his fall, I could not put Mac back together again.

That last road trip could have been filmed and sold as comedy, if it had not been such raw truth. On the way back to Florida, he started having hallucinations beyond anything I had witnessed before. Driving the Jersey Turnpike at seventy miles-an-hour, I held his flailing arm to stop him from thrashing around and doing bodily harm to both of us.

We spent the last night in South Carolina, just across the river from Savannah. I felt as though I was at home when we started to see the low country marshes. Dinner that night fed body and soul—crab that tasted like the kind we used to boil up after we caught them on a chicken neck tied to a string. I consoled myself with images of drifting in a rowboat out in these backwaters when I was in my teens. My friend Jesse could throw a shrimp net and haul in a boatload.

Jesse, why did you have to die so young? I miss you. We had such a good time out here in these rivers. I want to go back to that time. Hap, you taught me to

drive in your car here on these South Carolina roads.
When did it all end? This is really "low" country.
Can I rise from here?

We checked into a motel and I set out to get Mac settled in bed. I turned the TV on for him, took a deep breath, and gave thanks that we had both survived the ridiculous rocky trip down from New York. Confident that he was set for the night, I went downstairs to the spa. The whirlpool relaxed me and yet the anxiety about the next day's drive hovered over me as I sank deeper and deeper into the hot water.

This care-taking thing is over my head. Today this
trip has been too much. What am I going to do?
Not a nursing home—never! Who said, "Never say
never"? Damn them! Get yourself out of this tub,
buck up, and get back on the job.

I pushed the elevator button and, when the doors opened, there stood Mac in his plaid pajamas. He told some wild story about noise in the hall and a young girl who worked for the motel saying she would help him get back to his room. I never saw or heard from this "young girl" and have no idea if such a person ever even existed.

******

Mac had always encouraged me to sign up for college classes. The thought of this terrified me. This period came during the time when the Parkinson's was under control. He was even going back to the store in Quincy a few days each week and helping the new owner with some paper work. I felt free to come and go as I pleased, so taking classes was not out of the question. It just scared me.

They will find out how dumb I am—I can't possibly
take that chance.

Finally the day came when my need to "come out of the closet" with my writing overcame the fear. I braced myself and signed up for freshman English at the junior college. Taking the entrance exam was the most intimidating experience I had ever had. I was then fifty-seven years old.

My preparation for this big test was to spend two days fasting. Guess I thought "if Jesus did it when seeking divine direction, there must be some benefit." I briefly looked at a few English books with some rules of grammar and punctuation. I so wanted to write. I passed and was accepted for both English and Western Civilization.

Many of those on the faculty had been customers in one of our stores. They knew me well and this fact eased my "old-woman" freshman discomfort. I was surprised when a few other old folks showed up. I was not alone, but definitely a minority in this community of mostly nineteen-year-olds.

After that year, I was selected as a community newspaper columnist with *The Tallahassee Democrat*. Being published was the biggest validation I could ever get at that time. Success in business was nothing compared to having people read my words. It felt as though I was finally forming into the person of my dreams. I knew I could take no credit for this turn of events; surely some unknown hand was chiseling away. That feeling of being "sanded down" had come again. It felt as though all of me was exposed, right down to the bone.

One of my favorite articles explored my version of the creation myth and my view of Eve as a true heroine. She brought complexity and multi-dimensional reality into being. Life would have been so boring if we only knew "her good" without "her evil," I speculated on Eve's motivation. Once she had that piece of information, of course, she wanted companionship. She suggested that Adam try a tasty bite of awakening because with that bite she had discovered her need for relationship.

Sinful woman? Look again, fool.

This bit of unorthodox thinking caused a little stir with some of the fundamentalists in the area. I received a three-page letter from one such spokesman in West Florida, warning me in no uncertain terms that I was going "straight to hell" for espousing such "blasphemous ideas." He stated clearly that we all know Eve brought suffering and pain into this world and that the Biblical story was all about her disobedience.

Savoring every bite of that apple, I know the feeling. Fundamentalist, be damned. This story is about the complexity of life, about living fully. Get over your controlling rules!

I could have responded to him, but chose not to. I would have told him that men had been blaming Eve for their weaknesses as long as I could remember, starting with Adam's projections, "It was the fault of *that woman* you gave me." I was not going to take the blame for anything someone else thought I *made them* do.

To this day one of my favorite pieces of jewelry is a silver snake. On the days it is on my body, I find myself musing on the creation myth. The story tells me nothing of our history on this planet, but it speaks volumes to me about humanity. The frequent questions—Who am I? Why am I here?—keep circling around. I have yet to find answers, but love sitting silently with the questions.

The hostile letter writer was certain that I was headed for hell. He would not want to know that my idea of hell is the image of being stuck for any period of time with small-minded people certain that they have the answers to all of my unanswerable questions.

Mention the Baby

WHEN WE TUG AT A SINGLE THING IN NATURE, WE FIND
IT ATTACHED TO THE REST OF THE WORLD.

JOHN MUIR

AFTER DADDY DIED, MAMA MOVED into a retirement home in Savannah. This high-rise belonged to the city and, once again, she had the benefit of subsidized lodging. In her 80's and early 90's independent living was possible because Sister was close by. My brother Hap and I took up the slack with extra income for the niceties, the little extras like going out to lunch, beauty parlor visits and travel.

Group bus trips took her to scenic spots in the country. She was oblivious as to where they were on the map. When I would ask about where they went and what they saw, she would say, "You know, I just love scenery." There was no need to be bothered with mundane trivia such as location or historical happenings. Mayme did it her way—as always, she was in it for *atmosphere.*

Her women's "secret societies" had faded away and her circle of companions shrunk each year—a natural process. However, to Mayme this was an enormous loss—the flame of life was burning out. The group bus tours were not often enough, Mama needed her daily fix of people, lots of activity and familiar telephone conversations to stay up on all the gossip. Her own family could never fill this gap.

As she aged, it appeared she felt as though life had let her down. She drove me nuts with her repetitious banalities. Telephone conversations could have been conducted by pressing a button on a tape recorder that would re-replay the last call's lines. The script went like this:

Me: *Hey Mama, how you doing?*

Mama: *Just sitting here staring at these four walls.*

Me (caught between sadness and irritability): *Are you going out to lunch today?*

Mama: *Yes, but I am not hungry in the least—just something to do. I tell you, there's a difference between youth and old age.*

> *Mayme, you are past ninety, what the hell did you think would happen? Of course it is not like twenty-one. By the way, I am almost sixty now and your other daughter is over seventy—not like twenty-one either. Find a new line! This is not great wisdom you are spouting.*

I did not say what I was thinking, of course, as the conversation trailed on along the same mindless track. Finally, we reached the end of our lines, wished each other well and hung up. Now I am able to check "call Mama" from my "to do" list.

The conversation leaves me hanging with this question: "Could I change the steps of this dance?" I have no idea who is leading and who is following. I just know I would like some different music and a few new moves, and yet, I don't know how to do it. Is there any way I could engage her in conversation around a few of my favorite subjects, like maybe literature, religion, or relationships? Not likely. Such subjects are beyond her grasp in this long-distance, mechanical, tediously boring, obligatory weekly connection.

Questions raced through my mind:

Am I going to inflict this same torture on my child? Is there a life outside the sagging skin prison that many old women seem to see as their sole identity? Can I possibly be more than just my age? Do I continue as though I can keep up the pace that I established in my 30's or do I change my speed and give my energy only to activities that feed my soul?

Most of my life has been lived with my "cruise control" set at ten miles above the legal speed limit. In retrospect, I see how this tempo had the reverse effect. Speeding through life not only distracted me from feeling at home in my body. I seemed to live in the body of someone else from birth.

Mama dreamily drifted through her life as well as through my own. I see how we both could reach a sad ending by failing to accept and even feel the reality of age and our place in the moment. Her sister, Ethel, told a few stories about their experiences in boarding school that gave some clues to how Mama had chosen to live. Aunt Ethel was two years younger, but took on the role of the more responsible one. She said, "We had to sew our own dresses for graduation—the school required this. If I had not made Mayme's for her, she would never have graduated." She added that Mayme was far more interested in courting than she was in finishing school.

For one short time, when I was young, Mama had a job at Williams Seafood, on the beach road. Her sojourn into the world of restaurants yielded one marginal benefit—she discovered the secret of Williams' hushpuppies: tomato soup in the batter. We needed money and, instead, we got a recipe. I never knew why the job lasted only a few weeks. Apparently, taking responsibility—as in having income or getting an education—was not Mama's aim. Sadness washes over me as I picture this child-woman who missed out on so much just because her sights were set too low. She, like so many women born into similar circumstances, settled for a familiar second-rate existence.

To this day, I lack any ability to get into the mind of Mayme. When I was little and playing paper dolls with friends, I was a businesswoman. They were all mommies. My imagination worked overtime putting such a scene into place. Mayme never played that game. However, she did have an aunt who became my role model. Sometimes, Great-Aunt Esther came to Savannah on business, and stayed at the John Wesley Hotel. She was a tall, thin woman who wore smart-looking gabardine suits. Mama always went downtown to see her. I do not remember Aunt Esther ever setting foot in our Brady Street disorder. Mama never said anything about why she did not invite her to our house. It must have been a treat for her to meet in a ritzy place and hear about the family back in West Green—a reminder of the better life of her youth.

The game Mama seemed to play while living in the retirement home could have been called "fool the other residents." She read Harlequin romance novels, which she would hide inside a *Reader's Digest*. *The Inquirer* was also hidden inside the *Savannah Morning News* The reason for the deception was mainly because Mayme enjoyed her impish tricks. She seemed to think the folks in the day room cared that she read trash. Mostly it seems, she just got her kicks by twisting the ordinary into a parlor game. She missed her true calling as recreation director on a cruise ship.

In her early 90's, the decline began: Mayme lost all her hard-won coping skills. Out of her despair, she chose to go into the same nursing home where Daddy spent his last months. Medicaid picked up the bill. The facility was dreadful, even worse than our Brady Street home. Each time I went there, I would have to sit in the car and have a serious talk with myself before I could step inside. The scene was one of dementia, decay, stench and souls long dead with hearts that refused to stop beating.

I offered to move her to Tallahassee into a place that she might find more desirable—possibly a room with a view. That suggestion flopped. Mama was like her aunt who said of West Green, "This place is just the way Jesus left it and I want to stay right here, so he will know where to find me when he returns." Mama thought that the "Son of God" needed directions: she couldn't be found if she left Savannah. It was beyond my grasp why Jesus would choose Savannah or West Green for his return—oh well!

I hated the thought that this woman who had spent most of her life chasing after a fairy tale existence would have to end up spending her twilight years uncoupled and living in such a dump. Her years in the nursing home and Mac's Parkinson's intersected, and even though I managed to keep up my routine of travel and taking classes, their needs always loomed large. Guiltily, I shuttled back and forth to Savannah feeling a mixture of anger, shame and resentment. When Mac did not go with me, I was on the phone checking in just to make sure he had taken his meds or was not sprawled out on the floor from one of his repeated falls.

Being a caregiver was not natural to me; I never saw myself as a nurse. When I first began this uninvited career, I had a serious talk with god. I reverted to my idea of a god who would work things out to your liking if you phrased the request just right—words HE could understand, that "old-man-in-the-sky" kind of language. I told him that he needed to call someone else to fill this role; I was not the right person. A replacement never came, and I was stuck with this dreadful job.

Good friends, good wine, and frequent vacations kept me from running, screaming and pitching tantrums. Even with my nurturing limitations, I managed to excel for my twelve years as an unskilled practical nurse. That is the way I saw it, even though others might not have agreed.

Closure on my connection with the woman who birthed me did not come easily. I was left with swirls of fury and unclear thought. I wondered, "Was there some way I could have broken the code and found the storehouse of questions she was unable to ask?" I know there was so much more than that sad shell she disintegrated into after moving to the nursing home. I had no idea who this woman was before she became my Mama, who she might have been capable of becoming. My guess is that she saw Daddy as the Handsome Prince, and she clearly lacked the courage to face the truth of where that belief took her. I suspect, just like mine, theirs was a steamy courtship. She had to sneak out at night in order to have her illicit *rendezvous* with Sam. This deception must have taken them to shadowy places and brings up questions even I dare not ask. This boarding school Belle was never a woman I knew as my Mama. I cannot picture her climbing out the window of her room or hanging on to the ivy until she dropped to the ground to scamper off to their lusty meeting spot. A glimpse of that courage would have brought needed balance to the negative images that I have worked so hard to erase.

She was not that different from many women of her time, finding "the right man" was supposed to make all her dreams come true. And yet, the women of her time were the ones who fought the battle and won the right to vote. She never joined that rising tide. There were lots of women who *did* ask questions and fought to be heard when the answers were unjust. To my knowledge, that struggle and victory meant nothing to her. I wish I had quizzed her about that era. The Mama of my dreams would have been out front carrying the banner for women's rights.

If only—if only—if only—what?

On the day of Mama's funeral, my three siblings and I told stories—just what we knew of this ninety-six-year-old who had finally let go and crossed over to that other world, I know not where. Her last five years had been miserable. She was sick of living and mad with the world, and yet was obviously not ready to die. Getting old and infirm had not been her plan. Life had let her down. My sense is that her death brought her relief and certainly a greater sense of closure for the four of us—the sharing of memories helped.

Frances told us about the time the family went to visit Aunt Eva who lived out in the backwoods. These relatives were dirt-poor Georgia farmers. Aunt Eva's teen-age daughter had given birth, in spite of the fact that she had no husband. Sister would have been about twelve at the time—I had not yet been born. Low talk on the front porch about the shameful birth revealed the fact to my sister. She also heard how Aunt Eva planned to raise this child as her own.

Mama never had "facts of life" talks with her children; she felt helpless to be that direct. We just picked up information as best we could by listening in and then figuring out what it all meant. Frances had this "baby thing" all figured out when she was in the car *en route* to visit Aunt Eva. Just before their arrival at her house, Mama said, "Frances, when we get to

Eva's house, if you see a baby there, don't mention it." My brothers were in the car, but they did not remember hearing these instructions. This was "woman talk"—a subtle warning to Frances about what can happen to bad girls: They'll have babies that no one can ever mention.

Mama was the queen of cryptic. She gave new meaning to the word *unmentionable.* I have heard it used as a euphemism for women's undergarments—but a *baby*? Can you imagine? Like an infant covering their eyes, Mama truly believed that if you did not mention something, it did not exist. She must have considered this message to Sister as her only necessary sex education lesson.

Possibly Mayme never quite figured out the sex thing for herself. She frequently told me about the shock she felt when she realized she was pregnant with me at the very old age of thirty-six. Her tragic words were, "I thought about jumping in the river." Sister says that Mama was never overjoyed about the births of any of her four children. Choices for legal birth control were not plentiful, but the family was not Catholic, and after having a couple of babies, she might have figured out a way to keep those little tadpoles from finding their way in. She had no interest in facts, and I suspect she crossed her fingers—legs would have worked better.

I am certain Mama went to the grave with lots of mysterious messages floating around in her head—lots of *unmentionables.* Certainly Daddy's drinking had to be one. Her anger in those last years must have been the result of all those things she had stuffed—all those unasked questions. In her last years, I often asked if she needed to talk about something that might be troubling her. She would say, "I have lived this way so long; it is too late to change." The choice was hers. I am sure she would have said that she did not choose the anger.

Mama did not grasp the concept of "cause-and-effect." The word "dysfunctional" did not show up in her lexicon, either.

> *I so wish I could have known the Mayme who climbed out the window and slid down the ivy and ran off to meet Sam, her handsome lover. I think we could have been real buddies. I could have told her about Jay Helmken.*

In spite of the fact that I felt short-changed in the mothering department, Mama did teach me a few things. When I allow myself to look beyond my petty needs and desires, I see Mayme as the guide I needed, though certainly not the one I wanted. She held up the mirror, and taught me about choices, even when she seemed to be so unaware of the consequences created by the mindless choices she had made for herself. I realize she had no mentors, no lesson plans, and no intention to take on a maternal role, still, she was my torchbearer.

In a very convoluted way, Mama did manage to cope, even though it often looked as though she could not find her way, she still rose to most challenges with her gift for fantasy. The last years looked as though she had lost the battle and could not conjure up illusions and secret societies to transport her from old age and nursing-home hell. I wonder if I lack Mayme's imaginative ability to see the magical version of life as it flows. Maybe this was her final exam: keep heart beating, stay in miserable bed, complain to all who ask but don't really want to know, "How ya doin?" and, finally, don't forget to curtsy with a smile when death extends its generous hand.

It is an eternal mystery to me as to why shapeless souls keep living long past the time there appears to be a life force.

Maybe Mayme had to sew that damn dress herself that Aunt Ethel said was the requirement in order to graduate from the boarding school in Douglas, Georgia. Could she possibly have been stitching her life together in that abject and lifeless holding cell out in the marshes in Savannah? Mayme held on as a weaver of stories, spinning an endless wardrobe, not unlike her karmic sister, Scheherazade.

I would like to think those last years meant something in her long life—maybe the same way I hope my last years will give me high marks and a diploma.

Is this just my ego controlling me and trying to look good, to have on the smart-looking outfit and get noticed by the right guy? Is this the same old yearning, only this time with white hair and wrinkles in the picture? The idea of being a teenager trapped in an old woman's body is so ghastly to gaze upon—please, not me! If this is where I'll end up, then all my hocus pocus talk about transformation and contemplation becomes just another heap of mulch on my already-overflowing pile of rubbish. If all I have been doing is creating this narcissistic production, one with the final scene of a grand diva looking good on her deathbed, then I am as shallow as that girl who flew off to Paris concerned only about making her European debut. Will I ever be able to forgive myself for being, perhaps just a little bit, like Mayme?

This kind of fear caused my friend Rebecca to write a message around her mirror:

> OH, GOD, IF YOU LOVE ME,
> AS TIME MARS MY FACE,
> TAKE WILD DESIRES FROM ME,
> AT AN EQUAL PACE.

Giving up "wild desires" is easier for some than for others. I cling to mine and imagine that they will have to be pried from my clutching grasp when I finally let go and cross over. The last time I saw Rebecca, well into her 80's, she had a firm grip on her wildness—may I follow in her brave steps.

Do we ever get clear about this thing called desire and what drives us?

I feel as though I have had a metamorphosis over the past seventy years, but have I? There is great danger; it seems to me, in trying to figure out what milestones you have reached by comparing them to another. I think this journey calls us to keep our eyes straight ahead and not get hung up on where others are at the moment.

If I have any clarity now, it is that my journey has taken me where I needed to go. Feeling like an intruder from birth has brought a great and hard-won awareness to look within for acceptance. I know this lesson will never be mastered and I will never be a graduate of "the program." I still find myself yearning for a person or place outside myself to give me some sense of connection. Since Mac's death, I have made the leap into living alone and intentionally set out to stay with the loneliness. I choose less and less to look for an activity or another person to distract me. In many ways this feels like withholding from *myself*, and yet my deeper self, my spirit, is telling me this solitude is necessary for my ultimate well-being. Paradoxically, it feels right even when it can appear to be crazy-making.

This peace with aloneness seems to be missing in American culture. I rarely see evidence of its value in any media. I find books on the subject, but only a few fellow journeyers, like poets Mary Oliver and May Sarton, who share this cultivation of being. Instead, I see how the news that many are drawn to is the rise and fall of celebrities and their nutty behaviors, the quest for the right designer purse—anything to distract us from reflection by keeping us focused on the appearances outside ourselves.

Much of my life has been spent in this wheel-spinning cycle of wishing and wanting, anything different from the present moment. Wanting a family who was different from the one I had. Wanting a man who would open up and talk with me about something with more depth than headline news. Wanting a body that was thinner, younger, and more agile. Wanting more children. Wanting the good education I had missed. Wanting people to change their bigoted, warring ways. No matter how noble the wishes, they still seemed to keep me unsatisfied and isolated from my inner self, from my ability to be focused on the present moment.

The paradox for me was the fact that I began to make these discoveries about living "in the moment" by choosing to brazenly walk away from the world of surface satisfactions—to reject the state of affairs of that particular moment. I had to learn the lesson about making peace with myself by getting away from everything familiar. As fast as I could, I ran from a way of life that I had begun to hate. In retrospect, I see that I ran in the direction of finding my own lost self—that baby who came into the world raging about not being wanted.

Shamed by the unmentionable baby born out of wedlock to this niece, Mayme also felt humiliated by the fact that she got pregnant at the age of thirty-six. Her words, "I was embarrassed," reveal her worries that people were talking about her and the fact that she and Sam were still having sex. This thought made her want to kill herself.

I regret that I never rose tall enough to talk with Mama about this wall of pain wherein we both lived. The best compliment she ever gave me came the day she confessed, "If I had my life to live over, I would want to do the kind of things you have done." Finally, I was visible and affirmed—a holy moment. And I know that she was right, I have lived a blessed life with lots of enviable "atmosphere."

I hope she heard me on the day I told her what a good teacher she had been for me. That was as close as I could come to saying, "I forgive you for not wanting me." Her look told me this really puzzled her, but I knew I needed to say it, even if it was too late for us to have one of those Mother-Daughter "moments of truth."

Possibly, in the end, we both got the closure we needed. My acceptance of Daddy and his addiction, and the inevitable self-centered ways that follow, remain an open chapter. No matter how much I squint or flip the scene over in the looking glass, I cannot make his weaknesses and unconscious behaviors acceptable to me. It seemed to me that he had potential and just willfully refused to take responsibility for his actions.

When I first used the word *alcoholic* in talking about Daddy, my siblings acted as though I had given them a news flash of a tsunami coming. I was in my forties and damn sure by then that they knew the definition of alcoholism. It had never occurred to me they would be shocked.

"I never thought Daddy's drinking was a major problem," Sister said, as the spokesperson for all. She then went on, "Though I do remember one time when some men brought Daddy home from the woods when we lived in Stilson. He was drunk and just passed out on the floor where they left him. The next day, Mama said, "The reason your daddy got drunk was because ya'll needed school clothes and he had no money to buy them."

Say what—huh? Did I hear that right? It was our fault that our Daddy got drunk. How do I respond?

Sister was in her late 50's when she told this story. I just stared into her unblinking eyes and said, "Now do you get it, Sister? This is why you have spent your life feeling responsible for everyone else." Connecting these dots had not seemed to occur to her. I was the nutty one in the family—the one who thought about such trivial stuff—the one *needing* therapy. Sister told me once that the kind of things that interested me made her nervous.

The thought of accepting the excuse that my need for school clothes caused anyone to get drunk pisses me off to the point of wanting to take someone's head off. I grieve for my otherwise, very bright sister who accepted without question such a ludicrous explanation. That is another room in my vision of hell—to buy into lies and then spend your life believing them while trying to make this look like truth to others.

Sam lurked in the shadows of my life and my feelings about him continue to be fuzzy. I only hope I am done with him and he'll not rise up from that casket that I've refused to stare into. I want him to stay dead and buried—no extra innings—that game is over.

Postscript 2011

MY FIRST MEETING WITH THE publisher of this manuscript was scheduled in a place across from Forsyth Park. I parked at a coffee shop in the park and looked over at this trendy new spot in Savannah where I was expected to have a drink in the bar and talk about these words I had been struggling with for five years.

My god, that's Fox and Weeks Funeral Home.

For the first time since that memorable St. Patrick's Day in 1981, I was about to walk through those doors.

Please tell me I do not have to look in one of those boxes.

Fortunately, inside the door, I saw tables covered in white linens, floral arrangements, not funeral sprays and no corpses.

Dodged that bus another time.

So What?

YOUR LIFE IS WORKING, WHETHER YOU KNOW IT OR NOT.
SOMETIMES IT WORKS TO BRING YOU WHAT YOU WANT,
AND SOMETIMES IT WORKS TO KEEP YOU FROM WHAT YOU
THINK YOU WANT.

NEALE DONALD WALSCH

THE WORDS THAT I MOANED to my first therapist were, "I envy people who seem to be content with a life of social activities, dressing up for parties, playing golf—what is wrong with me?" He gave me his "don't be so stupid" look and replied, "Chris, you are *not* them." Imagine I am actually paying someone to tell me something so obvious. I should have been able to resolve that one. Therapy brought me face-to-face with my limitations, my ignorance, and yet, bit by bit, it also took away my desire to be like someone else. I got it: "I am *me*, not them."

When I was in the business of selling fashion to women, my least favorite question was, "Are *they* going to be wearing *this*, this year?" I would pause, take a deep breath, and remind myself that I could not insult this pathetic person if I wanted to stay in business. Again, because I liked that little *ka-ching* of the cash register, I would answer their query with as much enthusiasm as I could muster: "*Of course they* are, we saw it all over the market—it's really in." I wanted to say "just stand there in front of the mirror until you see yourself—your true self—the only one who can tell you what is right for you." Instead of lecturing to the customer, I said such words to myself. The voice coming back from my mirror eventually told me to go on the road and listen for further instructions.

It is so easy for me to see the patterns in this zigzagged route that I have taken over these seventy years, including the period in my life when I was the one asking, "Is this what they will be wearing this year?" I was unable to find the shut-off switch for that voice that nagged constantly about what I *should do* and how I *should* be more like someone else doing whatever they felt they should be doing. I could not see my own direction. I could only blindly follow or at least try to mimic the behaviors of those who seemed "together." I gave many people credit for having achieved a goal that seemed beyond my reach and, at the same time, criticized them for what I saw as a life without meaning or purpose. The trap snared me between these two opposing points of view.

My sharp edges and harsh judgment of others kept me locked in; freedom stayed one step ahead. When the boomerang of blame got thrown, it came back and, predictably, bonked me on my head. I could not connect my beliefs with my action. In theory I could talk about love and acceptance, but the true meaning of those words remained vague. I now know that I cannot act on a principle that I cannot see, taste, touch and feel. Above all, the vision is necessary before any change can happen.

I have no clear idea why I had the epiphany that caused me to pick up and leave everything that was familiar to step into an unknown world, why the wider image beyond the words appeared on my screen. Those of us who hear this strange call to jump into a void must be tuned into a radio station that others do not seem to pick up. There is no doubt in my mind that if people had a signal as strong as the one I received, they would go. I never felt that I had any choice in the matter.

The question for me then became, "Was I born with this particular wiring or did my life experiences program me to hear these particular instructions?" Of this much I am certain: If I had not changed the direction of my life and found clarity, I could not have kept any measure of sanity. The years of Mac's neurological hell, (that I might have to face myself, someday), would have done me in. Now, I have my own sanctuary within; the world of silence and solitude has shown me the way.

Back on Brady Street, Saturday mornings spent in front of the radio at Martha Faye's house listening to *Let's Pretend* might have been where thoughts of other worlds crept into my psyche. The program would begin with the Cream of Wheat jingle. We would sing along. "Cream of Wheat is so good to eat and we have it everyday." Those words transported us to the world of make believe. Cream of Wheat was Yankee food. We had never eaten Cream of Wheat—we ate grits. The stage was set for embarking upon mythical journeys. I felt myself going to faraway places and meeting folks other than the kids from Brady Street who went to 38th Street School.

I firmly believe the pilgrimage plan took its nascent form within me on Brady Street; when the time came to make my adventuresome dreams a reality, there it was. My time in convents, or driving through Navaho country, was as much fantasy as was Jack climbing up the bean stalk and finding a whole new world. I left the known world with its illusion of "happy family," and entered into a real, but unfamiliar reality of silence and contemplation. How sad is it that most of us live in the world of noise and never get to know who we *really* are? The *me* beyond a successful businesswoman and disgruntled family member has never been the one who goes through the motions of being the person someone else thinks is appropriate.

Arrogant and presumptuous as I am, I cannot say that I have come to the bottom of this search. There is no bottom. The "really real" is always one step away. The ultimate mystery of who we are and why we are here still dangles in front of me and gets my motor going everyday.

Mac—before Parkinson's—was fond of talking about the mysteries of life. In some ways, I suspect that he was supportive of my quest because he felt as though I brought edginess into our relationship that was out of bounds for him. He went so far as to say once, "I envy the freedom you seem to have that I lack." I treasure that memory. I loved those rare moments when he stepped out of his military control and investment mode and let me in to his raw truth—the guy I adored.

Our last move came eleven years after the one to Tallahassee and landed us in Asheville, North Carolina, where Mac died nine months later. The relocation to the mountains was a poignant journey together to a place where we both felt at home. For several years we had vacationed for the summer in the area and I had found a spiritual community that is still a very nurturing part of my life today.

On the morning when Mac took in his last breath, I was standing over him and just chattering away. I told him, "Greg, Kelly, Elizabeth, and Charlie are on the way and will be here soon." They were flying in from their home on the Persian Gulf, where they had been living for the past year. He knew they were coming and looked forward to greeting Greg with a salute. Greg now outranked him. Mac had retired as a

Lieutenant Colonel and Greg wore a Colonel's "bird" on his shoulder.

When I realized his breath had stopped, I stood for a long time with my hand on his head and continued to talk. I must have felt I could bring him back with words, the same way I had tried on those nightly calls while I was out west. I felt no panic, no rush to call for help. We had said all the things we needed to say. One of his last questions was to ask if all our bills had been paid; he was faithful to who he was right to the end. Our books were all balanced; the ledger could be closed. Over and over for the last weeks, we reminded each other that in spite of all the ups and downs of our life, we did truly love the other.

Before I made the call to hospice, I walked out on the balcony and stared off at the mountains. A feeling of gratitude washed over me. I gave thanks for help that comes from so many unexpected places and for life that is ongoing, even when I have had no idea where it is going. I was at peace—no questions—nothing was unfinished at that moment.

I walked back to the bedside for the final kiss good-bye. I did not try to hang on to him anymore than he did to me on that day when I left him in the kitchen with tears running down his cheeks. Life calls, as does death. There is no choice, we must respond.

Friends drove me to Charlotte to pick up my family. When they saw me waiting at the gate, words were not necessary. The message on my face said it all, "Papa is gone, and he chose not to wait for your arrival." There was no doubt in my mind; Mac made a conscious choice to spare them the scene of the deathbed vigil.

Elizabeth, age fifteen, and Charlie, about to turn twelve, adored their Papa, and the pain of their grief and loss pulsated through the Charlotte airport on that day. If I've ever had doubts about what life path they'll choose, all I have to do is pull up the picture of the two of them holding each other as they sobbed. Then, I know they are made of sound material. They might do odd things, just like me, like venture out without any idea where or why they are going, but they will be led by a stronger awareness—one of being connected with life.

There were funerals in Asheville and also back in Quincy. We sang "Take My Hand Precious Lord" and "Abide with Me", songs Mac asked the hospice music therapist for in his last days. Those words—"abide with me, fast falls the even tide, help of the helpless, oh, abide with me"—bring comfort and floods of memory. I cling to these memories—to lose them feels as though I would be robbed of my very being, of my very breath.

From Savannah to Paris to Asheville, and all the stops in between—my pilot, my lover, and my friend. Voulez vous coucher avec moi? Damn, I miss you, Mac!

Fitting all these pieces together to try to form a clear pattern has taken me up, down, and all around. What a ride it has been. As I look back on my circuitous route, I see the path has always been winding down—yes, down—away from my head to my heart. That voice asking the destructive questions, filling me with judgments, such useless habits is now in the background—still there but no longer believable.

When I think back to the time when I headed west *from* Mac and Quincy, Florida, it is hard for me to believe there really was any plan that I could count on to save me from the feeling of doom and destruction. Two months alone did not feel like a magic pill, nothing that would cure the ache in my soul. I just knew I had to leave; as much as I had also felt left by Mac's spirit. I stepped out on faith alone, even though there was no thought the leaving would do anything more than give me a little respite. Not faith in an outcome of my choosing, but faith that "the universe" – whatever that means – would somehow hold me up, would guide me, would teach me all that I needed to know for that day.

All this awareness comes only in retrospect. I could never see where I was going, only knew where I had been and that I had to leave it behind to find something different. I would never advise anyone to do as I have done. Such a decision must come from one's own inner urging, not from using my words as a manual. To tell another how to find their answers would be just like telling my customers, "Yes, buy that dress, because *it is what they will be wearing this year.*"

If my decision had been based on what *they* were doing, I would still be stuck in that awful prison of conforming to the status quo. I would still be waking each day to dread and boredom, trying to figure out what might ease the unbearable pain of keeping up the pace of my generation. I would be stuck with a yearning for which I had no words, only the language of blaming, martyrdom and despair—the feeling that someone caused this to happen, and I must find the guilty party.

My record of this kind of thinking is not yet wholly expunged. I still do more than my share of judging and blaming. As my people say, "I am fixin' to change my ways." I want to rise above this destructive pattern, but my plans and good intentions often pave the way to hell. Much of the time, I am fully conscious of the fact that I am not the person I intend to be. This mouth works faster than this brain—or wherever the place is from which unkind words emanate. Sometimes, I feel like I have to ask over and over: "Who is saying that?"

Who is using my voice? Oh shit, it is me! Is it possible to get to the place where those human frailties are left behind and I can act as a loving, accepting, kind person all the time?"

The answer does not come. I just know that, for now, I have to live with my higher self who flickers off and on unpredictably. This seems to be the tension of life; maybe it is what keeps us from defying gravity and just floating away. This much I do know—this grounding awareness is humbling and much more satisfying than my old predictable pattern of wishing and wanting.

That yearning for something beyond my reach now seems to be the gift I was given. If I had to define the urging, the pushing I felt in my soul, I would call it god. No other word seems to fit.

In my youth, I was hoping the day would come and bring me something more than I expected. On my infrequent visits back to Savannah, I would hope for a surprise encounter with Jay Helmken, not because I wanted to renew the old love affair, but because I would like to re-live the passionate feelings of riding on the back of his bicycle and listening to "Sixty Minute Man" together. This is the same feeling I get upon returning to Paris. The memory of being greeted by Mac at Orly, then waking the next morning in bed with him, brings a wonderful sense of belonging, of being special to one person, of being chosen. This explains why the language used in Song of Solomon, in the Old Testament, along with the poetry used by most mystics takes the form of erotic love; what better way to describe an unrequited *longing* for god? Because we are mortal and have only these bodies to house us, we are stuck with finite ways of describing the infinite.

For those two months of my pilgrimage, I seemed to find an in-between place. I traveled roads in Kentucky, New Mexico and California and, at the same time, some part of me soared outside those identifiable boundaries on the map.

There may have been other ways to reach the same conclusions, the same spot I stand on today, but the one I chose seemed to be the one that bore my name. The notion of being born with some map imprinted on the soul is intriguing to me. All around I see proof of this theory despite not having a logical defense for such experiences. Within families, there is such diversity. The fact, that with the same parents, one child chooses one path and another the total opposite. These differences must come from so much more than the environment or from nurture. There has to be some unique internal map inscribed in each of us.

Choice and courage appear to play a part. However, some people I meet seem to see their path the same way I do—no choice involved. There was a clear change in my ways of thinking that day my plan moved from the "want to" to the "must do." I did not make the shift by an act of courage; something outside my own ability to choose pushed me through that door.

It would be arrogant, even for me, to say, "god called and I answered." Those people who are so certain they have found god and recognize "the voice" scare the hell out of me. I only know that entering that "cloud of unknowing" felt overwhelming; I thought I would suffocate. Yet, I did not die. Instead, a sense of peace that made no sense came to comfort me. My mind wanted to sort it all out, categorize its patterns, find clear reason, but reason could not be found. No ordinary pattern appeared—loneliness vanished. I had no awareness that I had been hiding, yet, this time, it felt as though I had been found.

This description for my desert experience did not come at first. It has taken years for words to form. There was no booming masculine voice from above—the sort of biblical image many of us believe to be the way god's directions come. Instead, I experienced an inner quieting of my questioning voice, the one who had always prodded and poked me. A knowing came from beyond the place of merely finding the "right" answer.

I sought sanity, never certainty, let alone a god. My lifetime of yearning for something more, something unasked-for might have been the force that catapulted me out on this quest. Does thought really create reality? Did my unrequited spiritual longing conjure up this experience? Was I making little marks in my brain and then the day came when the dots connected and the roadmap popped up? I have accepted that I will never know. Thinking about possibilities can keep me shifting those colorful glass images in that kaleidoscope of my brain and then leave me speculating for the balance of my life.

This search for sanity never ends.

The Beginning

I KNOW NOT WITH WHAT WEAPONS WORLD WAR III WILL BE FOUGHT, BUT WORLD WAR IV WILL BE FOUGHT WITH STICKS AND STONES.

ALBERT EINSTEIN

JANUARY 2007

My seventieth birthday came and, of all things, I have planned another pilgrimage—this time to Italy. Just like the last one, some inner voice told me to go—why Italy? I guess the answer is the same one given by folks who climb mountains, "Just because it is there." One thing I am hoping will happen is a burst of creative energy for more writing. A change of scenery, hanging out with people who speak a different language may cause a rupture in some of those hardened places in my brain. I am on a quest for new words, new thoughts and new habits.

May 2007 will be the third anniversary of Mac's death. That first year, I only felt the liberation from my caregiver's job. I traveled and caught up on all the things that I had missed for the couple of years before, when life had become a too-often tedious routine connected with Parkinson's disease. I was left with only the images of the frail Mac: the one who fell each time he tried to walk in that last month, the one who was confined to a hospice bed and, at the end, needed more and more morphine to blunt the pain. I did not miss *that* Mac. The next year, my grief and loss took me down and then came the gut-wrenching loneliness. Memory began to return of the Mac before Parkinson's. Memories of my business partner, my traveling companion, that man who could make me laugh. Then, as I began to do some writing, the memories of the difficulties in our relationship came into relief. Try as I might, no hiding place could be found. The most difficult part was sorting through the information and deciding what was *my* story to tell and what part belonged only to Mac and Greg. I could not depend on anyone to validate the authenticity of my words. My message was coming from within and had only to be *my* story, *my* truth. Here, I found myself stuck with this new brand of aloneness.

There was no one there when I awoke in the morning. I had to resort to audio books to make me think that I had a friend reading to me so that I could fall asleep. At dinner each night, the table was set for *just one*. Going out to eat felt unbearably lonely, every place was filled with couples. The word *just* always preceded *one*. When I walked into a restaurant and asked for a table I'd hear the familiar, insensitive query: "*Just one* for dinner?" "Thanks for the reminder!"

As much as I value my solitude and freedom, this foreign single life felt more like abandonment, like something vital was missing, as though a part of my body had been amputated.

Forty-seven years earlier, I had moved from my parents' house at age twenty into an apartment in Paris with Mac. I had no experience of the solitary life. I did not wake up and face this new era with ease or with any plan. I went kicking and screaming into "widowhood." I hate that word. It sounds pathetic, not at all me. That's a framework I refuse.

Acceptance of change did not just magically happen. I think of myself as a flexible person, but flexing to the point life required of me felt as though I would break wide open. It felt more as if I were trying to force my foot into a too-small shoe or convincing myself that I loved the taste of mincemeat. The adjustment required effort, hard work and self-invention. Staying with the discomfort was tedious and non-negotiable.

Elizabeth, my granddaughter, came to Asheville to go to boarding school, so I was not without family. Then there was my large circle of friends. My day continues to begin with meeting to meditate, then having coffee and great discussions with these dear friends. To the untrained eye, I might look like someone who had all her needs for companionship met. But, to me, it feels as though the cosmos has made a swift shift— would my equilibrium ever return? Did I ever have such an anchor?

Early on, I learned to be gentle with myself and not to lay guilt on just because I was not able to find my way. I would tell myself that I could invite friends to dinner each night, but that required energy and often I had little. Also, I knew they would not fill the gap in my life. I could not bring back a time when activity, an identified role and sense of purpose just came with the day; when I did not have to map out or even think about each step.

The plan to hang out in Italy, this new call to step out again into the unknown, felt different from that other pilgrimage. Then, I was *escaping* a situation beyond my understanding and looking for something to save me since my familiar "savior" was all but gone. This time, I was not fleeing a prison; it's more like running *towards* something. What that target is I have no idea.

Friends tease me about finding a lover, but that's not even close to my plan. I do not fit the profile of the rich American dowager on the prowl. Tony, the steward from that long ago flight to Paris was not awaiting me in Rome. Unlike then, this time I give no thought to my wardrobe for the Atlantic crossing. Jeans have replaced the black sheath and the houndstooth duster. Supportive walking shoes now take precedence over style—I still choose the cute ones though.

There is almost no one whom I feel a need to explain my plans to—my family seems to be at peace with any decision I make. This time, I wish there was a place I could run to where war did not tag along. Though TV does not come into my home and I take no newspaper, I still manage to hear the death counts around the world—especially the sites of U.S. occupation. If only there were a spot of peace on the planet where news of death and destruction did not seep in, most surely, I would go there.

If I could put my head under the pillow, as Mac's mother used to do when there was a thunderstorm over Quincy, I would do it. She would line up her four boys on the bed and tell them, "Be still." She believed that lightning was attracted to noise. She would then stay under the pillow with the quiet little boys huddling beside her until the danger had passed.

I would love to have my little boy beside me until this violently irrational storm blew over. Instead, he is in-and-out of war zones and I am still searching for some means by which I can "let it be." If I thought that I could shield Greg, (and all the sons and daughters of those mothers out there), I would not only use it, I would spread the good news. My wish is to line them up on the bed and just be quiet until meanspirited, violent ways come to an end.

In the last few days, I have heard news of furious Italians against the Iraq war and our use of their country to house U.S. troops. They were protesting U.S. presence and pushing to get our military bases out of their country. I may be jumping into a hornet's nest with my plans for this upcoming pilgrimage—but that may be where I belong for now.

The art in Italy beckons; I could worship at the feet of Michelangelo's *David*. I reject much of the interpretation, such as that "big man god," depicted in the creation story on the ceiling of the Sistine Chapel, yet, it feeds my soul. My god is the god of creation. What's new? What is changing? I no longer worship that "capital g" god. My god is a "lowercase g," one I encounter in the ordinary, the everyday, in the burning bushes of folks I meet and every wild image that floats through my head. I no longer go to church, partly because I hate the triumphal, conquering language used in the services. I understand the god of evolution—my own evolution and the evolution of each being on this planet.

Creation being birthed each day gets my motor going and gets me out of bed. *That* I can sing praises to (even if I cannot carry a tune). Well, at least I can dance to it. And, as Emma Goldman says, "If I can't dance to it, it's not my revolution."

JUNE 2007

This pilgrimage is similar to my other one sixteen years ago, except there is little temptation to communicate with anyone. I live in an apartment on Lake Como, make a daily run to the local grocer, walk along the lake at sunset each evening and the rest of my day is spent writing or reading. My basic needs are all met.

The books that keep me company are two by Thomas Merton: *Peace in the Post Christian Era* and *The Inner Experience*. Both were published after his death. I'm not sure of the significance, but somehow it seemed they were important for me to live with for this summer. Other than those, I read a few novels.

As I sit at the word processor each day, life slows down so much. Someone might have to take my pulse to make sure I am still alive. Could this be an indication that my life is drawing to a close? Does the pulse just slowly wind down? I remember those days when, like Lily Tomlin, all I wanted to do was to find evidence that there was intelligent life on the planet. Now it is clear to me that my own pulse is the only one I have the right to take—all else is not my business. This kind of non-attachment would have sounded totally self-centered to me when I began my quest for life in 1991.

As the Zen saying goes:
"When we discover that the truth is already in us, we are all at once our authentic selves."

Now, in 2007, it seems to be the basic fundamental truth. Is there some line I crossed that brought me to this awareness? Is this the aging process? I care about others, but know I am not called to evaluate or assess their life force. Occasionally I slip up on this one and eventually; I forgive myself once again.

The "Old Me" thought I was responsible for bringing light to all, sort of like Joan of Arc leading the battle. At least I had to be out front carrying the torch. That arrogant piece of me did not give up easily, she had to be wrestled down and will occasionally try to rear up and take charge. The best teachers of humility have been my grandchildren. When Greg was growing up, I thought it was my responsibility to give him all the lessons he needed. Now I know how misguided that thinking was. Whatever he learned, he learned *in spite of me*, the same way I have learned the important lessons in my life.

Try as I might though, I cannot escape the physical frailties that can come with old age. When I walk on the cobblestone and steeply-inclined streets, I am focused on each step. My self-image would be destroyed if I returned home in a wheel chair—some images will never leave us. I am stuck with my "I-can-take-care-of-myself" attitude. White hair, I can live with, but please not that feeble, bent over, old-woman image.

My hope is that when I return to the States at the end of this pilgrimage, I will be willing to rest in the new awareness and move yet another step into maturing with grace. My much larger wish is that these crazy wars will end and I will see humankind taking a step forward into a new, peace-seeking and sustaining Renaissance. Surrounded by all the art produced by Italian visionaries, I believe in the possibility that we can have a collective awakening. Like The Hundredth Monkey story, maybe if some of us change our destructive, egocentric ways, soon all will change and, miraculously and simultaneously, peaceful ways will become second nature.

For now, I am stuck with reports of global cruelty and righteous vindictiveness getting worse. The recent news of terrorist activities floods my computer screen. I cannot run far enough to avoid the headlines, but the choice to isolate myself and turn off the screen is not one I am willing to make. My contemplative life is not one of shutting out the world, rather, it is a desire to bring the world in and to be willing to see and embrace *reality* as it is—truth.

In that first year after Mac died, I went with a group out into the Sinai Desert. There were about fifteen of us, some from my meditation community and others who shared our interest in "desert spirituality." We visited the ancient monasteries, sometimes bedding down there and other nights we slept out under the stars in our sleeping bags. There, I connected with the first Christian hermits who wrote of the inner experience of god. All I have to do now is close my eyes and I can return to that awareness of the presence of those monks who knew, instinctively, the path they were called to follow. My time there gave me a glimpse of my global connection with desert pilgrims (and possibly a cosmic one) as I bedded down on the sand and gazed at the heavens.

As I seek this ultimate oneness with life, I am not without the awareness that this mysterious longing is exactly the search that led me into darkness—where it seemed as though there would never be light again, no hope for finding even a little ray of sunshine. As awful as those times were and as much as I would have done anything I could to consciously avoid them, I now know that those were the times that led me to my present unexpected treasures. There was no way I could have navigated myself to such a spot—the Paraclete, that unseen helper, had to have a hand in my flight that eventually landed me on more solid ground.

To paraphrase Rumi on the subject,

THIS DRUNKENNESS BEGAN IN SOME OTHER TAVERN,
AND WHOEVER BROUGHT ME HERE WILL HAVE TO COME
AGAIN AND TAKE ME HOME.

I certainly found myself in a tavern not of my choosing, and had no idea how I happened to end up there. My days in northern Arizona and New Mexico were a different tavern, and some invisible guide did come to lead me home, a new home. The way back to the old one was no longer visible. It was as though that path had become overgrown and, even if I wished to find it, I no longer had access.

Still, my game of hide-and-seek does not end. A winner does not emerge. It is still not clear who is doing the hiding and who the seeking.

And so it is.

Author Bio

CHRIS MCMILLAN GREW UP IN Savannah, GA and now lives in Asheville, NC. Her life journey has included traveling the world with her husband Mac during his Air Force career and then for twenty years they were business partners in retail shops. At the age of fifty-four, she stepped out into a new world and followed an inner voice that took her on a ten thousand mile journey that she labeled her search for sanity.

Now at the age of seventy-four her passion, other than writing, is meditating, yoga, gardening, good food and friends to share it with around her table.

Contact her through *chrismcmil@gmail.com*